Fighting for Freedom

Blacks in the
American Military

Lucent Library of Black History

Fighting for Freedom

Blacks in the
American Military

Lucent Library of Black History

Other titles in this series:

Fighting for Freedom

Blacks in the American Military

Lucent Library of Black History

Gail B. Stewart

LUCENT BOOKS

An imprint of Thomson Gale, a part of The Thomson Corporation

Detroit • New York • San Francisco
New Haven, Conn. • Waterville, Maine • London

For more information, contact
Lucent Books
27500 Drake Rd.
Farmington Hills, MI 48331-3535
Or you can visit our Internet site at http://www.gale.com

LIBRARY OF CONGRESS CATALOGING-IN-PUBLICATION DATA

Stewart, Gail, 1949-
Blacks in the American military / by Gail B. Stewart.
    p. cm. — (Lucent library of Black history)
Includes bibliographical references and index.
ISBN 13: 978-1-59018-952-8 (lib. : alk. paper)
ISBN 10: 1-59018-952-3 (lib. : alk. paper)
1. African American soldiers—History—Juvenile literature. 2. African American veterans—History—Juvenile literature. 3. United States—Army—African American troops—History—Juvenile literature. 4. United States—Armed Forces—African Americans—History—Juvenile literature. 5. United States—History, Military—Juvenile literature.
I. Title.
E185.63.S695 2006
355.0089'96073--dc22   2006026417

Printed in the United States of America

Contents

Foreword

It has been more than 500 years since Africans were first brought to the New World in shackles, and over 140 years since slavery was formally abolished in the United States. Over 50 years have passed since the fallacy of "separate but equal" was obliterated in the American courts, and some 40 years since the watershed Civil Rights Act of 1965 guaranteed the rights and liberties of all Americans, especially those of color. Over time, these changes have become celebrated landmarks in American history. In the twenty-first century, African American men and women are politicians, judges, diplomats, professors, deans, doctors, artists, athletes, business owners, and home owners. For many, the scars of the past have melted away in the opportunities that have been found in contemporary society. Observers such as Peter N. Kirsanow, who sits on the U.S. Commission of Civil Rights, point to these accomplishments and conclude, "The growing black middle class may be viewed as proof that most of the civil rights battles have been won."

In spite of these legal victories, however, prejudice and inequality have persisted in American society. In 2003, African Americans comprised just 12 percent of the nation's population, yet accounted for 44 percent of its prison inmates and 24 percent of its poor. Racially motivated hate crimes continue to appear on the pages of major newspapers in many American cities. Furthermore, many African Americans still experience either overt or muted racism in their daily lives. A 1996 study undertaken by Professor Nancy Krieger of the Harvard School of Public Health, for example, found that 80 percent of the African American participants reported having experienced racial discrimination in one or more settings, including at work or school, applying for housing and medical care, from the police or in the courts, and on the street or in a public setting.

It is for these reasons that many believe the struggle for racial equality and justice is far from over. These episodes of discrimination threaten to shatter the illusion that America has completely overcome its racist past, causing many black Americans to become increasingly frustrated and confused. Scholar and writer Ellis Cose has described this splintered state in the following way: "I have done everything I was supposed to do. I have stayed out of trouble with the law, gone to the right schools, and worked myself nearly to death. What more do they want? Why in God's name won't they accept me as a full human being?" For Cose and others, the struggle for equality and justice has yet to be fully achieved.

In many subtle yet important ways the traumatic experiences of slavery and segregation continue to inform the way race is discussed and experienced in the twenty-first century. Indeed, it is possible that America will always grapple with the fallout from its distressing past. Ulric Haynes, dean of the Hofstra University School of Business has said, "Perhaps race will always matter, given the historical circumstances under which we came to this country." But studying this past and understanding how it contributes to present-day dialogues about race and history in America is a critical component of contemporary education. To this end, the Lucent Library of Black History offers a thorough look at the experiences that have shaped the black community and the American people as a whole. Annotated bibliographies provide readers with ideas for further research, while fully documented primary and secondary source quotations enhance the text. Each book in the series explores a different episode of black history; together they provide students with a wealth of information as well as launching points for further study and discussion.

Stuggling for the Right to Fight

The second-class status of black Americans can be traced back to the first delivery of African slaves to the North American continent in 1619. As slavery grew and became integral to the economy —especially in the South—the relationship between blacks and whites worsened. Because slaves were viewed as property that could be bought and sold, most whites considered them inferior in intelligence, talent, and human worth. And even after slavery was officially outlawed in the nineteenth century, these racist ideas endured and were reflected in virtually every aspect of American life.

No, and Yes

The pervasive belief in white superiority meant that the answer to most requests from the black community, whether for voting rights, or the right to integrate an all-white school, or to have equal opportunity in the workplace, was "No." For centuries, black Americans who wanted to serve in the armed forces were refused, too—for a variety of reasons. During the Revolutionary War, for example, one widespread objection to black slaves serving in the military was the fear of arming a group of people who could turn those weapons on their white masters. For much of the twentieth century, the objections were founded on long-held beliefs that blacks were incapable of carrying out the difficult tasks demanded of soldiers.

Whatever the reasons behind them, the military establishment's refusals to admit blacks into the ranks never lasted for long. Leaders who were reluctant at the beginning of a conflict to allow black Americans to serve in uniform begrudgingly relented as it became clear that more soldiers were needed to achieve victory. As a result, black soldiers have fought in every American war.

But permission to serve in the U.S. military came with severe impediments for black Americans. They were often the most poorly equipped and often were not even provided the same quality of uniform as white soldiers. As recently as World War II, black Americans were not allowed to be marines or air force pilots. They could join the navy only as workers in the mess. The

During World War I, black recruits at Camp Meade in Maryland were assigned uniforms that were generally inferior to those issued to whites.

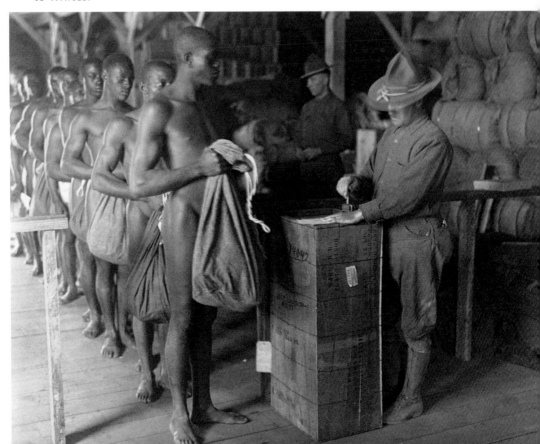

army allowed some black soldiers to fight, but only in all-black regiments, usually led by white officers.

War on Two Fronts

In spite of this humiliating treatment, however, black Americans did join the military, and fought and died in battles in the United States and around the world. Ironically, many perished fighting for rights and liberties that neither they nor their children nor their grandchildren would enjoy. The attitude of military leaders, noted black poet Paul Lawrence Dunbar in 1898, was basically, "'Negroes, you may fight for us, but you may not vote for us. You may prove a strong bulwark when the bullets are flying, but you must stand from the line when the ballots are in the air.'"[1]

With little or no support from the military establishment or their white comrades in arms, black soldiers fought battles on two fronts, facing danger, violence, and suffering at the hands of their own countrymen as well as the army they were fighting. But despite such abuse, a great many black soldiers conducted themselves with a spirit of courage, dignity, and amazing heroism. The story of the black experience in America's wars demonstrates the depth of that spirit.

Chapter One

Fighting for Someone Else's Liberty

Although very little has been written about them, blacks made many notable contributions to the American colonies' fight for independence from Britain in the eighteenth century. Though colonial leaders at first disagreed about whether to allow blacks to enlist in the Continental army, thousands of men of color eventually did join. Blacks fought in every major battle, from the first at Lexington and Concord to the final one at Yorktown. Historians say that one of every seven soldiers in George Washington's army was black.

It is not surprising that many blacks—both freemen and slaves—were eager to join the colonists' side against the British. For years before the war actually began in 1775, excited talk about liberty and freedom from British rule was common in the colonies. To the segment of society who had no freedoms, the notion of a new life of liberty was especially attractive. Many enslaved blacks of that day hoped that helping the colonists win independence would lead to their own release from bondage.

Militias and Minutemen

In September 1774, seven months before the first shots of the war were fired, representatives from each individual colony met to decide the best way to deal with the growing threat of British aggression. This assembly, known as the Continental Congress, decided that each colony should create a system of militias that could defend towns and cities, utilizing 25 percent of the available men in an area. In addition, certain elite forces, called minutemen, would be also be established. Their name came from the fact that these groups had to be capable of responding at a

Colonial soldiers fought British troops at the Battle of Lexington in 1775. The clash marked the beginning of the American Revolution.

minute's notice, for no one knew when the first act of aggression would come.

Black freemen in the north were eager to join the militias as well as the minutemen, and there are records of a few northern slaves who joined, too, as assistants to their white masters. Southerners, by contrast, refused to allow blacks to serve. One reason was that allowing slaves to leave the plantations to serve in militias would be an economic hardship because there was no one else to perform their work. However, a far more important reason for the South's refusal was the worry that giving slaves weapons would enable them to easily start a rebellion. In the South, where slaves outnumbered white owners, the possibility of such an uprising was frightening. One group of slaveholders noted that "there must be great caution used, lest our slaves when armed might become our masters."[2]

Answering the Call to Arms

The militias had not been in place for long when the war began, as predicted, near Boston, where the largest contingent of British forces was stationed. Suspecting that the colonists had a stockpile of weapons in Concord or nearby Lexington, about sixteen hundred British troops began to move on April 19, 1775. Paul Revere and other patriots sounded the alarm, and when the British arrived in Lexington, they were met by armed minutemen. Shooting between the two forces lasted only a few minutes, and the British marched on to Concord, where more than 130 militia and minutemen were waiting. This battle was more involved, and the British suffered substantial losses.

Although officers tended not to mention black soldiers in their battle reports, historians know that some of the minutemen at Lexington and Concord were black. The name of Prince Estabrook, described only as "a Negro man" who was wounded at Concord, appears on a notice listing casualties after the battles. Estabrook, a slave from Lexington, is the only name on the list that does not have "Mr." preceding it.

Heroes at Breed's Hill

Soon after the battles at Lexington and Concord came the battle at Breed's Hill, sometimes called the Battle of Bunker Hill. After this battle, two black militia soldiers received more than simply a passing notice from their commanding officers. Breed's Hill was the bloodiest battle of the entire war, as cannon fire pelted both armies. Participants later wrote that the hill, which overlooked Boston Harbor, was so slippery with blood that many of the men had difficulty keeping their balance.

A twenty-five-year-old slave named Peter Salem, who had already fought at Concord, was one of fifteen hundred militia troops under the command of Colonel William Prescott at Breed's Hill. Salem and his fellow soldiers waited as British major John Pitcairn, who had commanded the forces at Lexington and Concord, led his assault on Breed's Hill. Concerned about their scant supply of ammunition, Prescott had warned his troops not to shoot "till you see the whites of their eyes."[3] When the British got within fifty yards (2,286m) of the militia, Salem and the others opened fire, driving the British back. However, after a few moments, the militiamen were forced to retreat because their ammunition was

Salem Poor at Breed's Hill

■

Among the heroes at the Battle of Breed's Hill in the early days of the Revolutionary War was a twenty-eight-year-old free black named Salem Poor. He showed extraordinary courage during the fighting, and afterward fourteen officers petitioned the general court of Massachusetts to honor him.

The Subscribers begg leave to Report to your Honorable House, (which Wee do in justice to the Caracter of so Brave a Man) that under Our Own observation, We declare that A Negro Man Called Salem Poor of Col. Frye's Regiment—Capt. Ames. Company—in the late Battle . . . behaved like an Experienced officer, as Well as an Excellent Soldier, to Set forth Particulars of his Conduct Would be Tedious. Wee Would Only begg leave to Say in the person of this said Negro Centers a Brave & Galant Soldier. The Reward due to so great and Distinguished a Caracter, We Submit to the Congress.

Quoted in Ray Raphael, *A People's History of the American Revolution: How Common People Shaped the Fight for Independence*. New York: New Press, 2001, p. 282.

almost gone. As Pitcairn jubilantly shouted that the British were once again victorious, Salem stood his ground and shot him.

One British officer later praised the American troops, recalling "an incessant stream of fire from the rebel lines. . . . Most of the [militia] . . . the moment of presenting themselves lost three-fourths and many nine-tenths of their men."[4] An American militiaman wrote in his journal of "a Negro man belonging to Groton, took aim at Major Pitcairn, as he was rallying the dispersed British troops and shot him thro' the head."[5] Salem was singled out for his bravery, and a group of American officers later rewarded him by formally presenting him to General George Washington.

Left Out of a New Army

The members of the Continental Congress followed the news of the early battles. Though they were pleased that the militias had done as well as they had, it was clear to them that the recent clashes with the British were not isolated incidents. War was inevitable, and local militias, no matter how brave, were no substitute for a real army. The Congress voted to establish a Continental army made up of soldiers from all of the colonies. A colonel from the Virginia militia, the forty-three-year-old Washington was chosen as the new army's commander-in-chief.

With the formation of the Continental army came some new dilemmas. Many of the congressional leaders were uneasy with the inclusion of freemen and slaves in the Continental army. Some believed that even though blacks had performed admirably as minutemen, many white soldiers—especially those from the South—would refuse to serve with them. Others worried that black soldiers might not be as brave or capable as white soldiers. And there was also the widely held opinion that the colonies should not allow slaves to serve in the army because their contribution would be, according to the Congress, "inconsistent with the principles that are to be supported, and reflect dishonor on this Colony."[6] In other words, it would be hypocritical to allow men who were not free to fight for the freedom of whites.

Washington himself was against the idea of blacks in his army. As a slave owner, he felt that the inclusion of black soldiers might be divisive. After getting input from his war council as well as the Continental Congress, Washington finally decided to issue a directive that "Neither Negroes, Boys unable to Bear Arms, nor old men unfit to endure the fatigues of the campaign, are to be enlisted."[7]

An Offer from the British

Protests against this directive immediately arose, both from blacks already serving in militias and more than a few white officers. General John Thomas wrote a letter to John Adams, an important Massachusetts congressman, insisting that to exclude black soldiers from the new army was a big mistake. "In the regiments at Roxbury," wrote Thomas, "we have some Negroes; but I look on them, in General, Equally Serviceable with other men . . . many of them have proven themselves brave."[8]

Thomas's views on allowing blacks in the Continental army did not change the minds of the American military leaders, but the words of Lord Dunmore, the Royal Governor of Virginia, did. Dunmore issued a proclamation that promised freedom to any slave who volunteered to fight with the British army: "And I do hereby further declare all indented Servants, Negroes, or others . . . that are able and willing to bear Arms, they joining His Majesty's Troops as soon as may be, for the more speedily reducing this Colony to a Proper Sense of their Duty, to His Majesty's Crown and Dignity."[9]

Dunmore felt certain that many of the slaves would immediately run to the British, thereby collapsing the entire Southern economy. In fact, within three months after the proclamation, thousands of slaves had indeed attempted to escape their homes to offer their services to British military units. Many were recaptured, only to try again to escape. Dunmore's proclamation thus not only hurt the colonial economy but convinced many blacks throughout the colonies that their only chance at freedom was tied to the success of the British army.

Some slaves were so desperate get away to the British that they fought their white owners. In Maryland, a Dorchester County court decided to deal severely with three slaves who had killed a white man in their rush to join Dunmore. To frighten other slaves into thinking twice about escaping, the three men were sentenced to a grisly public execution: "[E]ach of them to have their right hands cut off and to be hanged by the neck until they were dead; their heads to be severed from their bodies and their bodies to be

General George Washington, pictured here leading the troops to winter camp at Valley Forge, allowed black freemen to join the Continental army.

divided each of them in four quarters and their heads and quarters to be set up in the most public places in the county."[10]

On Second Thought

In addition to the stir caused by Lord Dunmore's proclamation, another occurrence helped convince Washington and his war council to allow black soldiers to fight with the Continental army: an increasing shortage of soldiers. Many of the soldiers' initial terms had expired, and they felt that they were needed at home. Their farms needed tending, and their families could not last long without them. Besides, there had been very little fighting after the first three battles of the war, and many of the American soldiers were restless. One Massachusetts soldier wrote to his wife, "Our People are all most Bewicht about getting home."[11]

To fill the ranks with more soldiers was crucial, for Washington knew there would be much more fighting soon. He advised the Congress to order each colony to send more militias to replace those soldiers who were leaving. This time, black soldiers were allowed to enlist if they were freemen. Slaves were officially banned, but local recruitment boards had quotas to fill, and often looked the other way when slaves accompanied their masters into the army. Sometimes, too, a slave might be permitted to take the place of an owner who was not interested in going to war. As a result, many whites who had never owned a slave purchased one simply to take their places in the draft. And although white enlistees were given property or a monetary bonus, many slaves were promised that they would be freed when the war ended.

The Life of a Soldier

As a result of these measures, by the summer of 1776 there were black soldiers in almost every battalion of the Continental army. One soldier in the British army commented in his journal, "No regiment is to be seen in which there are not Negroes in abundance; and among them are able-bodied, strong, and brave fellows."[12] While some did fight on the battlefield, many of these black soldiers spent more time in support roles than in actual combat. They drove wagons and delivered supplies, dug graves, and sometimes served as servants to officers.

Some, like James Armistead, were valuable spies. Armistead was assigned to the French general Lafayette, who accompanied a large French force to help the Americans in 1781. As part of his service Armistead traveled back and forth between the American and British encampments in Virginia. He was able to convince the British officers that he was spying for them, while he was actually a double agent—gathering intelligence for the Americans. Lafayette later testified, "His intelligence from the enemy's camp were industriously collected and more faithfully delivered."[13]

No matter in what capacity a soldier served, however, life as a soldier in the Continental army was difficult. The food supply was often scarce, and the supplies that did arrive at camp were

As a spy against the British, James Armistead (at right) was invaluable to the French general Lafayette.

often spoiled. The soldiers lacked boots, blankets, and warm uniforms. Often they went months without pay. And these hardships affected black and white soldiers alike.

The First Rhode Island Regiment

Although the vast majority of black soldiers served in integrated units, a few all-black units received a lot of attention during the Revolutionary War. The most famous by far was the First Rhode Island Regiment, led by one of Washington's best young officers, Christopher Greene.

The regiment was created in 1778, following the loss of twenty-five hundred soldiers to disease and lack of provisions

"Starvation and Death for Their Wages"

■

The slaves who joined the British army in hopes of attaining their freedom were often treated inhumanely. One of the most vivid examples occurred at Yorktown, the final battle of the war. As the British were under siege, supplies ran dangerously low, and rather than share food equally with everyone, they cut the rations of the black soldiers. At first, those soldiers were given the spoiled biscuits and rotted meat that none of the whites would touch—and when that ran out, the starving soldiers were driven away from the camp toward the American army.

Joseph Plumb, a young American who kept a diary during his years as a soldier, recalled his shock at seeing many black soldiers sent away from the army they had joined:

> During the siege, we saw in the woods herds of Negroes which [the British general] Lord Cornwallis (after he inveigled them from their proprietors), in love and pity to them, had turned adrift, with no other recompense for their confidence in his humanity than the smallpox for their bounty and starvation and death for their wages. They might be seen scattered about in every direction, dead and dying, with pieces of ears of burnt Indian corn in the hands and mouths, even of those that were dead.

Quoted in Ray Raphael, *A People's History of the American Revolution: How Common People Shaped the Fight for Independence*, New York: New Press, 2001, p. 269.

after a long winter at Valley Forge, Pennsylvania. Rhode Island was unable to recruit enough whites to meet its assigned quota, so its state legislature made a very attractive offer to its black population: "It is Voted and Resolved, that every able-bodied negro, mulatto, or Indian man-slave in the State may enlist . . . to serve during the continuance of the present war . . . [and] that every slave so enlisting shall, upon his passing muster by Col. Christopher Greene, be immediately discharged from the service of his master or mistress, and be absolutely free."[14]

The regiment was called into battle in August 1778, soon after its formation, to fight a mercenary army of German soldiers in the only battle waged in Rhode Island. Although the black troops lost the battle, they inflicted five times more casualties on the enemy than they received. In fact, the regiment put up such incredibly fierce resistance that the commander of the professional German army in that battle refused to make his men fight the next day—and he himself asked for a transfer to another post.

One white veteran of the Battle of Rhode Island described the First Rhode Island's participation:

> There was a black regiment in the same situation. Yes, a regiment of negroes, fighting for our liberty and independence—not a white man among them but the officers—stationed in the same dangerous and responsible position. Had they been unfaithful, or given way before the enemy, all would have been lost. Three times in succession were they attacked, with most desperate valor and fury, by well-disciplined and veteran troops, and three times did they successfully repel the assault, and thus preserve our army from capture. They fought through the war. They were brave, hardy troops.[15]

Promises Kept, Promises Broken

Although observers in both armies similarly praised the courage of black troops, the outcome for black soldiers after the war was mixed. Some slaves whose liberty had been guaranteed by the state did acquire their freedom, such as those who served in the First Rhode Island Regiment. And many slaves who had fought for the British were taken to Nova Scotia and Jamaica, where they were released as freemen.

However, there were thousands whose dream of freedom was never realized. The British took many to the West Indies, where they were sold to new masters or distributed as payment to British officers. Many slaves who fought on the American side found that owners who had sent them to fight in their stead—with the promise of freedom afterward—had not provided a written guarantee, and as a result reclaimed the soldiers as slaves after the war. In a bitter irony, although they had shed blood in the war for freedom, these men could not reap the rewards of their sacrifice.

Chapter Two

Fighting Against a Way of Life

Despite the fact that black soldiers had fought admirably during the Revolutionary War, blacks were not welcomed by either the Union army or the Confederate army at the outset of the American Civil War. Though ultimately blacks served just as heroically in this war as their forebears had in the struggle for independence against the British, once again they first had to convince the nation to give them a chance to fight. What made these circumstances so ironic was that more than any other segment of the population at that time, blacks had a very personal stake in the outcome of the conflict.

"It Will Become All One Thing, or All the Other"

The war began over the issue of states' rights, particularly with regard to the institution of slavery. In the years since the Revolutionary War, the Northern states had abolished slavery, but it was firmly entrenched in the South. There, slaves provided unpaid labor, and Southern plantation owners were well aware that the economy of the South would quickly collapse without it.

As the calls increased for slavery to be abolished throughout the nation, tension grew between the North and South. Of primary concern were the new states entering the union, such as

Kentucky and Missouri—states that lay between the slave states of the South and free Northern states. The North wanted to make slavery illegal in any new state, but the South disagreed, saying that each state should decide the issue for itself. The arguments were passionate, and the anger became more heated.

Abraham Lincoln, who was elected president of the United States in 1860, had warned that the issue of slavery would tear the nation apart. "A house divided against itself cannot stand," he said in 1858. "I believe this government cannot endure, permanently half slave and half free. I do not expect the house to

Part of the new confederacy, South Carolina attacked Fort Sumter on April 13, 1861, beginning the Civil War that pitted North against South.

fall, but I do expect it will cease to be divided. It will become all one thing, or all the other."[16]

His prediction was correct. Believing that the election of Lincoln, who was decidedly antislavery, meant the federal government would be no friend to the Southern plantation owners, South Carolina seceded from the union. That state was followed by six more, and the new Confederate States of America was formed as a separate nation in February 1861. Two months later, on April 12, 1861, South Carolina attacked Fort Sumter, a Union stronghold—which officially put Americans at war with one another.

No Black Soldiers for the South

No one in the North believed that the war would last longer than a few months. In theory, at least, the South was at a huge disadvantage. For one thing, the white population was just a little over 8 million, compared to almost 19 million in the North. In addition, the North had a great many factories where weapons and war supplies could be manufactured, as well as farms that grew food. In the South, there were few factories or farms producing food. Mostly, the South was made up of plantations where only cotton was grown.

Yet even though their chances of victory seemed small, Southerners would not consider arming any of the 4 million slaves in the South to fight for the new confederacy. Most whites did not want to lose their free labor, and just as Southerners had in 1775, they worried that weapons in the hands of slaves would be turned on their owners. As was true before the Revolutionary War, there was the widespread belief that blacks were incapable of being effective soldiers. Finally, many Southerners agreed that it would send a strange message for the Confederacy to have blacks fighting for white slave owners. Senator John C. Calhoun of South Carolina remarked, "The justification of slavery in the South is the inferiority of the Negro. If we make him a soldier, we concede the whole question."[17]

The South did, however, draft thousands of slaves into the war effort to perform menial labor. They were to help with construction, do cooking, dig latrines, and generally serve as camp workers. They would not carry weapons of any kind and wore tags signifying what regiment they served. So critical was this slave labor pool to the war effort, in fact, that historians say that it was set up before the first white soldiers were drafted.

"Do You Know That This Is a White Man's Government?"

Blacks were no more welcome in the Union army than they were in the Confederate army. As soon as the war began, many black Americans flocked to enlist. In New York, black leaders themselves offered to spend the money to arm and assemble three black regiments. The black community in Philadelphia offered to

Abolitionist and African American leader Frederick Douglass strongly advocated blacks serving in the Union army.

assemble two more, and in Washington, D.C., more than one hundred men tried to enlist. After all, many of them felt the war was about slavery, and no one had a greater interest in the outcome than black Americans.

The U.S. War Department turned down all of these offers. One reason was that no one in the federal government believed that

"It Was Indeed a Time of Times"

---∎---

In *American Patriots: The Story of Blacks in the Military from the Revolution to Desert Storm*, author Gail Buckley describes the anticipation and reaction throughout the North as people heard for the first time that President Lincoln had really freed the slaves.

On New Year's Day, 1863, churches and meeting halls throughout the North were packed with people awaiting official confirmation of Emancipation. When the news finally came on the [telegraph] wire, sometime after ten P.M., a one-hundred-voice choir broke into the "Hallelujah Chorus" at Boston's Tremont Temple, where Frederick Douglass [and other notables] were waiting, and where a human chain had been formed to the telegraph office. In Dracut, Massachusetts, Adrastus Lew, Underground Railroad conductor and Revolutionary descendant, and his wife were hosting an integrated party when the news was rushed in. They immediately formed a "Peace and Unity" club and decided to meet every year thereafter.

On the fiftieth anniversary of the Proclamation, in 1913, [one black minister who witnessed the event] . . . recalled original Emancipation events in Washington. "Men squealed, women fainted, dogs barked, white and colored people shook hands, songs were sung and . . . cannons began to fire at the navy-yard, and follow in the wake of the roar that had for some time been going on behind the White House. . . . It was indeed a time of times . . . nothing like it will ever be seen again in this life.

Gail Buckley, *American Patriots: The Story of Blacks in the Military from the Revolution to Desert Storm*. New York: Random House, 2001, p. 88.

the war would last very long. In fact, because of the South's apparent weaknesses, Lincoln and his aides put out a call for seventy-five thousand men to join the Union army—and this enlistment was for only a brief ninety-day term. There was no need, they believed, for black soldiers.

This decision provoked a great deal of criticism from the black community, especially from Frederick Douglass, the most eloquent black spokesman of that time. Douglass complained, "Colored men were good enough to fight under Washington, but they are not good enough to fight under [General George B.] McClellan." He predicted, "The side which first summons the Negro to its aid will conquer."[18]

Despite such predictions, many government officials believed that to allow black soldiers into the Union army was a mistake. Governor David Tod of Ohio felt that white soldiers would not wish to serve alongside blacks, and as a result the unity of the army would suffer. "Do you know that this is a white man's government," he asked, "[and] that the white men are able to defend and protect it; and that to enlist a Negro soldier would be to drive every white man out of the service?"[19]

"This Is No Time to Fight with One Hand"

As the war proceeded without black enlistees on either side, the Confederate army surprised the North. On July 21, 1861, not long before the ninety-day enlistments for the Union soldiers ran out, the Confederate army soundly defeated the Union army at Bull Run, Virginia. As a result, though he did not believe allowing blacks to enlist as soldiers was a good idea, Lincoln felt it was important to increase the size of the Union army. He permitted fifty thousand black men to join to perform noncombat duties, just as the South had done with slaves.

Many observers in the North believed that Lincoln and his War Department were foolish for not taking advantage of thousands of men who were willing to fight. John Andrew, the governor of Massachusetts, said that it seemed clear that the war was not going to be as short as predicted, and that the color of a man's skin should make no difference in wartime: "It is not my opinion that our generals, when any man comes to the standard and desires to defend the flag, will find it important to light a candle, and see what his complexion

This 1866 engraving shows jubilant crowds of African Americans in Washington, D.C., celebrating Abraham Lincoln's Emancipation Proclamation.

is, or to consult the family Bible to ascertain whether his grandfather came from the banks of the Thames or the banks of the Senegal."[20]

In fact, some generals were already arming blacks who crossed Union lines to approach their armies. One of these was General James Lane, who despite the objections of the War Department included an all-black force among the regiments he organized to defend Kansas. Another general in the field who openly defied the federal government was John Fremont of Missouri, who declared that any slave who joined his army would be freed—a promise for which Lincoln relieved Fremont of duty temporarily. Many slaves escaped from their owners to join Fremont.

Douglass continued to pressure the government into rethinking its policy on black soldiers. He argued that the North would lose the war unless it could use all of its strength to fight the Confederacy—and blacks were a key part of that strength. "This is no time to fight with one hand, when both are needed," he said. "This is no time to fight only with your white hand, and allow your black hand to remain tied."[21]

Lincoln felt the pressure of public opinion, as well as pressure from his own generals, who were concerned by the disappointingly low number of soldiers enlisting by the fall of 1862. The president had long maintained that as long as slavery existed, the states could never be united, and on New Year's Day, 1863, he formally acted to remedy the situation. On that day, he issued the Emancipation Proclamation, which freed all slaves in the Confederate states. In the text he proclaimed that all persons of "suitable condition will be received into the armed service of the United States."[22] The government's ban on black troops was over.

"Men of Color, To Arms"

In the wake of the announcement, the Union army rushed to create new black regiments, as well as to arm blacks who had been limited to a supportive role in the war. Douglass and other black leaders enthusiastically embraced the task of recruiting young men to join the all-black regiments being formed. Douglass gave a stirring speech in March 1863, in which he shouted, "Men of color, to arms," and told his audience that "liberty won only by white men would lose half its luster."[23]

Ulysses S. Grant, commander of the Union army, was extremely pleased at the prospect of new soldiers. "By arming the Negro," he wrote President Lincoln, "we have added a powerful ally. They will make good soldiers and taking them from the enemy weakens him in the same proportion they strengthen us."[24]

Black regiments were started up from states such as Iowa, Rhode Island, Connecticut, Pennsylvania, Illinois, Ohio, Michigan, and Indiana. The most famous of them all, however, was the thousand-man 54th Massachusetts Infantry Regiment. As were all black regiments, the 54th Massachusetts was commanded by a white officer—in this case, a twenty-five-year-old abolitionist named Robert Shaw. The regiment was the first organized in the North after the Emancipation Proclamation, so it captured the public interest like no other. When the 54th Massachusetts paraded through the streets of Boston on its way to the front in May 1863, the city was crowded with throngs of curious spectators—both black and white. The *Boston Evening Journal* reported on the scene:

> No regiment on its departure has collected so many thousands as the Fifty-fourth. The early morning trains from all directions were filled to overflowing, extra cars were run, vast crowds lined the streets where the regiment was to pass, and the Common was crowded with an immense number of people, such as only the 4th of July or some rare event causes to assemble.[25]

"How I Got Out of That Fight Alive, I Cannot Tell"

After training and doing support work for other army regiments, the 54th Regiment finally got its chance to fight on July 18, 1863. Union army leaders wanted to take control over the port of Charleston in South Carolina. However, to do that, they had to overpower Fort Wagner, which stood on an island at the entrance to the harbor.

The 54th charged at dusk, storming behind the color sergeant, who held the large American flag aloft. In those days the flag of an army was such an important symbol during war that it was crucial that it never fall to the ground during a battle. Soon into the 54th Regiment's charge, the color sergeant was shot, and another member of the 54th, a young sergeant named William Carney, hurried to take the flag. Shaw was killed, but the 54th fought on. Armed with bayonets, the regiment was no match for the cannons and huge naval guns of the fort. One soldier recalled later that the bloodshed was horrific: "Men fell all around me," he said. "A shell would explode and clear a space of twenty feet, our men would close up again, but it was no use—we had to retreat, which was a very hazardous undertaking. How I got out of that fight alive, I cannot tell."[26]

Unbelievable, too, was the fact that Carney managed to keep the flag aloft. Though he was shot three times and was severely wounded, he staggered into the medic's tent, uttering words that became famous throughout the Union army: "Boys, the old flag never touched the ground."[27] Because of the courage he displayed in that battle, Carney became the first black soldier ever to receive the Medal of Honor.

As the all-black 54th Massachusetts regiment attacked Fort Wagner in Charleston, South Carolina, in 1863, Sergeant William Carney held the flag.

Almost half of the 54th Massachusetts were killed, wounded, or captured during that battle, and ultimately the Confederate army was able to hold Fort Wagner. Even so, the regiment had made a name for itself. After the battle, no one doubted that black soldiers could fight.

Separate and Unequal

Yet while the Union claimed to be pleased with the way black soldiers conducted themselves on the battlefield, the army's treatment of those same soldiers told a different story. For example, no matter how well trained and competent black soldiers were, they were almost never promoted as highly or as frequently as white soldiers. And even after black regiments displayed bravery and heroism in encounters with the Confederate army, they still spent the majority of their time doing backbreaking labor that white troops were rarely asked to do.

Perhaps the most glaring difference, however, was in the wages that black and white soldiers were paid. The lowest-ranking white soldier received $13 per month plus a clothing allowance of $3.50. When black soldiers were allowed into the army, they received $10 with a $3 clothing allowance deducted from that wage. And while white soldiers were given pay raises for time served and promotions, black soldiers—no matter how long and well they served, or at what rank—never received any pay increase.

Black soldiers, their white officers, and those who had called for black inclusion into the army were outraged at the situation. Corporal James Henry Gooding of the 54th Massachusetts, in a letter to Lincoln, asked, "Now the main question is, are we soldiers, or are we laborers? We have done a soldier's duty. Why can't we have a soldier's pay?"[28] Eventually, under pressure from Lincoln and state leaders, Congress finally enacted legislation in 1864 that guaranteed equal pay for black and white troops.

Victims of Hatred and Violence

In addition to inequities in pay, promotion, and battlefield experience, black soldiers faced more deadly problems. Soon after the North began allowing black regiments to fight, the Confederacy announced that any black Union soldiers captured in battle would not be treated as regular prisoners of war. Instead, they would be considered either runaway slaves (even though many were freemen) or insurgents—and as punishment, would be shot. In addition, the Confederate congress passed a law stating that all captured white officers of black regiments could be executed.

Lincoln responded with his own announcement: For every white Union officer or black soldier killed while captive of the Confederacy, a Confederate captive would be shot. Nonetheless, Confederate soldiers committed atrocities on many battlefields during the war, killing black soldiers who tried to surrender rather than taking them prisoner. One of the most infamous examples is the massacre carried out in April 1864 against soldiers at the Union's Fort Pillow in Tennessee. Led by General Nathan Bedford Forrest, more than 1,500 Confederate troops stormed the fort, which was manned by about 550 Union soldiers, many of whom were black. Black soldiers who tried to surrender were savagely butchered—many were buried or burned alive. The

In 1864 at Fort Pillow in Tennessee, Confederate troops viciously slaughtered Union soldiers, most of whom were black.

final death toll was 231 and included black women and children staying at the fort.

According to Forrest's report, the Mississippi River was "dyed with the blood of the slaughtered for 200 yards." In that report, he expressed the hope that "these facts will demonstrate to the Northern people that the negro soldiers cannot cope with Southerners."[29] Condemned throughout the North, the Fort Pillow massacre galvanized black troops to use "Remember Fort Pillow!" as a rallying cry from then on.

Making the Ultimate Sacrifice

Although few black soldiers experienced violence as extreme as that at Fort Pillow, they were nonetheless treated poorly in countless ways by the armies on both sides. Yet despite the obstacles they faced, many succeeded admirably—and often heroically—on the battlefield. By the end of the war, there were 186,107

The Heroics of Robert Smalls

One of the most famous black heroes of the Civil War was a South Carolina seaman named Robert Smalls. He was taken to Charleston and made the pilot of a Confederate ship called *Planter*. Smalls had no intention of remaining a slave and planned to make his escape quickly.

Late on the night of March 13, 1862, when the *Planter* was loaded with weapons to be delivered to a nearby fort and the captain and other white officers were sleeping in Charleston, Smalls quietly smuggled his wife and young children aboard. With the Confederate flag flying from the mast, Smalls put on the overcoat and hat worn by the captain and set out to sea. When he safely passed the other Confederate ships blocking the harbor, he put up a white flag of truce and turned his ship over to a Union vessel anchored just outside the blockade.

Smalls was taken to meet President Lincoln, who thanked him for his bravery and the contribution of the *Planter* to the Union cause. The ship was used throughout the war to ferry a black unit, the South Carolina Colored Volunteers, along the coast to various raids they conducted in Georgia and Florida. Smalls was made a captain in the Union navy, and after the war was elected to the U.S. Congress.

Civil War hero Robert Smalls sits for a portrait in 1860. Smalls escaped with his family from South Carolina during the war.

black enlisted soldiers. They had participated in 449 engagements with the enemy, 39 of which were major battles. There was no doubt that black soldiers had made the ultimate sacrifice, as had many white soldiers. Just a little under one-third of the black soldiers had died in the war.

Among all the things that black soldiers could be proud of was the role they played in ending slavery for all black Americans. Liberty for all was now the law of the land. The future must have looked bright for those soldiers and their families. The reality, however, would prove to be disappointing—not only for black civilians, but for those who wished to serve in the military.

Chapter Three

Over Here and Over There

The federal government determined that there was still a need for an army after the Civil War. Although hostilities between North and South had ended, the American people faced dangers in the years afterward. The government decided to maintain an army of about fifty-six thousand men, and blacks were allowed to serve in it. In fact, one in five soldiers after the Civil War was African American and served in one of four black units that were active in the postwar years.

Buffalo Soldiers

Soon after the end of the war the westward movement in the United States began in earnest. Each week more and more Americans were heading west, not only as settlers but as workers laying railroad track and erecting telegraph lines. The soldiers stationed west of the Mississippi River were charged with protecting those in the western frontier—usually from Native Americans, who objected to the whites taking their land.

Although there was a great amount of hostility between the U.S. soldiers and the Indians, the Indians had a deep respect for the black cavalrymen, whom they considered brave and tenacious fighters. The Indians called them "Buffalo Soldiers" because the men's dark scalps and short, coarse hair reminded them of the buffalo, which was sacred to them. Over time, the term came to be used for all black cavalry troops.

But while the Buffalo Soldiers received respect from the Indians, they got little from army officials. They were almost always given the most dangerous assignments and were usually issued the worst equipment and gear. For example, white troops were provided with comfortable, well-fitting uniforms, but the black soldiers often were not. One white soldier described a typical group of Buffalo Soldiers on horseback:

> Most of the men ride in their blue flannel shirts. . . ; some of the men take off their shirts and ride in their gray knit undershirts. There are all sorts of hats worn, of American and Mexican make, the most common being the ugly army campaign hat of gray felt. . . . There are few trousers not torn or badly worn, especially in the seat. [Some troopers even exchange their army blues for civilian overalls.] Here is a man with a single spur; here one without any.[30]

Jim Crow and Disappointment

Though they were not treated well, the Buffalo Soldiers often received praise from follow soldiers and their white officers who observed their performance in combat. When four regiments of the Buffalo Soldiers were sent to Cuba to fight in the Spanish-American War in 1898, a white officer admitted that he was amazed at their ability to fight. "I must say," he said, "that I never saw braver men anywhere."[31]

Such praise was worth nothing back home, however. As Buffalo Soldiers returned from their tour of duty—either from the western frontier or from the war in Cuba—it was clear to them that the emancipation and freedom Lincoln had promised African Americans had definitely not arrived. Racial discrimination was everywhere—but was especially prevalent in the South, where racial inequality was a legal way of life. Southern states had enacted the so-called Jim Crow laws, which restricted the rights and privileges of African Americans—from making it illegal for blacks to use public water fountains or restrooms to designating what school their children could attend and in which neighborhoods

Buffalo Soldiers, always assigned dangerous duties by the army, ride across the Arizona desert as they head west.

they could buy a home. No matter how heroically a black soldier had fought for the United States, he was viewed with distrust or even outright hatred in the South. There were countless incidents of returning African American soldiers in uniform being thrown out of restaurants or bars, being refused service in stores, and denied seats on streetcars.

Historians say that in many ways the discrimination in the South was worse for black soldiers than for black civilians. Since the time of the Revolutionary War, the idea of an armed slave or freeman in their midst was terrifying to many Southerners, and to them the sight of Buffalo Soldiers and other black troops in their uniforms was an affront.

A Pioneer at West Point

In 1877 a twenty-one-year-old named Henry O. Flipper became the first black man ever to graduate from the prestigious American military academy West Point. Born into slavery in Georgia, Flipper and his family became free before the Civil War, when his father, a shoemaker, purchased their freedom.

Flipper was a bright, inquisitive boy. Although in those days school was out of the question for most black children—especially in the South—Henry's father paid a woman to tutor him, and he did well at his studies. Flipper was thrilled when his application to West Point was accepted. He knew going in that it would be difficult and was prepared for being a social outcast among the white cadets. He made it a point to be forgiving of their racist remarks and cruel comments and to act as his parents had taught him, as a gentleman. He wrote:

> One must endure these little tortures—the sneer, the shrug of the shoulder, the epithet, the effort to avoid, to disdain, to ignore. . . . If I cannot endure the prejudice and persecution, even if they are offered, then I don't deserve the cadetship, and much less the commission of an army officer.

Henry Ossian Flipper, *The Colored Cadet at West Point: The Autobiography of Lieut. Henry Ossian Flipper, the First Graduate of Color from the U.S. Military Academy*, New York: Johnson, 1968, p. 291.

The young Henry O. Flipper, the first African American graduate of West Point, poses for a portrait in his cadet uniform.

"It Was the Best Piece of Work I Ever Witnessed"

The black troops coming home from the war in Cuba were especially at risk when their troop trains passed Southern cities. One train carrying young African American soldiers stopped in the middle of the night in Nashville, Tennessee. As the soldiers slept, two hundred civilians and seventy-five police officers, armed with guns and clubs boarded the train and attacked them. A white sheriff who took part in the beatings recalled later how exciting the assault was: "It was the best piece of work I ever witnessed. . . . The way they went for the Negroes was inspiring. . . . And if a darky even looked mad, it was enough for some policeman to bend his club double over his head."[32]

The same hostility was shown throughout the South, though not always as violently. Black soldiers recalled being spit at, called names, and threatened as they walked down the street in uniform. In Tampa, Florida, a white officer of a black regiment wrote to his wife: "This is not a nice town for my men. The feeling is strong against their color."[33]

To Fight? To Refuse to Fight?

Considering the humiliation and mistreatment they received, it is not surprising that when President Woodrow Wilson declared in 1917 that the United States would enter the world war to help the Allies (France and England), many African Americans were reluctant to participate. The black newspaper *Messenger* published an editorial urging black men not to enlist: "We are conscripting the Negro into the military and industrial establishment to achieve this end for white democracy four thousand miles away, while the Negro at home, though bearing the burden in every way, is denied economic, political, educational, and civil democracy."[34]

On the other hand, black leaders and writers such as W.E.B. DuBois believed that World War I was an opportunity for black Americans to lead the struggle for equality at home while fighting for democracy in Europe. He urged them, "while the war lasts, to forget our special grievances and close our ranks shoulder to shoulder with our own white fellow citizens and the allied nations that are fighting for democracy."[35]

In the end, hundreds of thousands of African American soldiers did enlist, heeding DuBois's optimistic ideas. However, it

W.E.B. Dubois, who championed equality for American blacks, urged African American men to fight during World War I.

soon became clear that the discrimination experienced by black soldiers in past wars had become even more serious. Though the U.S. Army needed the numbers the black soldiers provided, it was unwilling to provide them either with support or respect.

"Men Died like Sheep"

As was true in earlier wars, black troops were poorly equipped compared to their white counterparts. For example, in army camps where soldiers went for training before being shipped overseas, the white soldiers were given new-issue uniforms, while the black officers were often forgotten. Sometimes African American troops were even given old Civil War uniforms, much to the amusement of the white soldiers. "When one of the organizations thus clad marched through the camp," one historian wrote, "it became the laughing-stock of the rest of the soldiers, and the men were humiliated."[36]

More serious were the living quarters provided at U.S. camps. Black troops were not permitted to sleep in barracks as white soldiers were, but were forced to sleep instead in tents, without stoves for heat. This proved disastrous for many young black recruits at Camp Alexander, Virginia, during the winter of 1917–1918, when the lack of warm clothes, blankets, and stoves resulted in a large number of deaths. In a 1918 report to the secretary of war, an officer reported that during that winter, "men died like sheep in their tents, it being a common occurrence to go around in the morning and drag men out frozen to death."[37]

The assignments the men received proved to be one of the biggest disappointments of all. Many blacks had enlisted to fight, but instead of being slated for combat duty, they were once again expected to perform menial labor—building roads, cooking, cleaning, and driving supply trucks. These jobs were not the sort that would help them advance or prove themselves as a valuable asset in the war effort. In fact, of the two hundred thousand African American troops sent to France, only forty thousand saw any combat at all.

Handing over Troops to the French

The black combat units who were sent to France presented a problem for U.S. military leaders. Brigadier General Lytle Brown, the director of war planning, was not convinced that blacks would conduct themselves well in battle and also worried that it would be difficult to keep white and black troops separate in the field. Since integrating the army was not even a consideration, Brown and other U.S. military leaders were not sure what to do with the black soldiers.

To sidestep the issue, they decided to loan large contingents of African American troops to the French, who had lost more than two hundred thousand soldiers since the war's beginning. French commanders, desperate for replacements, were overjoyed to add the black soldiers to their army. And because the French did not have a history of racial discrimination, the black Americans were more than willing to be part of French fighting units.

Ironically, however, as it became clear that the French and the African American regiments were a good match, the American military leaders became worried. They noticed that the French treated the blacks as equals—a development that they felt would be a great problem when the troops eventually returned home. The African

Black soldiers wear the Croix de Guerre medals the French military awarded them for bravery during World War I.

Americans almost certainly would think that they should be treated the same way in the United States. Just as certainly, white Americans —especially those in the South—would never stand for that.

A Secret Memo

To "help" the French understand the best way of dealing with the African American soldiers, U.S. leaders created a document, entitled "Secret Information Concerning Black American Troops," that outlined how the French should treat the black American soldiers and why. "Although a citizen of the United States," the document explained, "the black man is regarded by the white American as an inferior being with whom relations of business or service only are possible." The black man, it said, has vices which "are a constant menace to the American who has to repress them sternly." The document continued, warning the French that it was dangerous to be too familiar or friendly with blacks: "We may be courteous and amiable with these . . . but we cannot deal with them on the same plane as with white American officers. . . . We must not eat with them, must not shake hands or seek to talk or meet with them outside the requirements of military service."[38]

The document was denounced by the French government, who promptly passed a resolution in the National Assembly to condemn such prejudice and affirm the equality of all, no matter what class, religion, or race. As it turned out, the African American soldiers got along well with the French, who were touched that so many of the American soldiers learned to speak their language. The French military was impressed with the bravery and courage shown by the African American troops—heroism that they witnessed almost immediately on the battlefield.

The Hellfighters of Harlem

The first group of African American troops that came to the front were members of the 369th Infantry Regiment—most of whom were from the Harlem section of New York City. The 369th soon experienced the horrors of trench warfare, in which the German army and the French army traded artillery and machine-gun fire from their trenches. These were often no more than forty or fifty yards (37 or 46m) apart, with barbed wire strung along their length for protection.

Members of the all-black 369th Infantry Regiment fight from the trenches during a battle in Germany during World War I.

It was in this setting that two members of the 369th showed how courageous the soldiers from Harlem could be. Privates Henry Johnson and Needham Roberts were on sentry duty one night soon after arriving in France. They were on guard near the no-man's-land between the two trenches, making sure no German soldiers tried to cross through the barbed wire nest to kill Allied soldiers.

Johnson and Roberts heard the sound of wire clippers. They shouted a warning to their fellow soldiers back in the trenches, and began throwing grenades at the patrol of twenty German soldiers. Both men were wounded, but continued to fight. Roberts threw grenades at the raiding party, while Johnson struck several soldiers with the butt of his rifle. As two Germans tried to take

Roberts prisoner, Johnson attacked them with his bolo knife. The frightened Germans retreated, and the Allied soldiers—except for Roberts and Johnson—were unhurt.

Because of their heroic efforts to keep their fellow soldiers safe from the German raiders, Johnson and Roberts received one of the highest military honors bestowed in the French army—the Croix de Guerre. The 369th soon became famous for its brave, tireless soldiers, for they remained at the front for 191 consecutive days—a length of time almost unheard of during World War I. And while Johnson and Roberts were the first to win French war medals, they were not the only members of the 369th who did. More than one hundred men in that regiment were awarded the Croix de Guerre or the even more prestigious Medaille Militaire (military medal). And because of their fierceness with bayo-

German Appeals to Black American Troops

Germany used propaganda as a weapon in World War I, dropping leaflets attempting to make African American troops less willing to risk their lives fighting for the United States. Following is an example of this German propaganda:

Do you enjoy the same rights as the white people do in America, the land of Freedom and Democracy, or are you rather not treated over there as second-class citizens? Why, then, fight the Germans only for the benefit of the Wall Street robbers and to protect the millions they have loaned to the British, French, and Italians? You have been made the tool of the egotistic and rapacious rich in England and in America, there is nothing in the whole game for you but broken bones, horrible wounds, spoiled health, or death. . . . Let those do the fighting who make the profit out of this war. Don't allow them to use you as cannon fodder. To carry a gun in this war is not an honor, but a shame. Throw it away and come over into the German lines. You will find friends who will help you get along.

Quoted in Kai Wright, *Soldiers of Freedom: An Illustrated History of African Americans in the Armed Forces.* New York: Black Dog & Leventhal, 2002, p. 134.

net and bolo knife, the African American infantrymen of the 369th were called "Hellfighters" by the German soldiers, who came to fear them.

The Black Swallow of Death

Another African American who won French medals was a pilot named Eugene Jacques Bullard. Born in Georgia, Bullard saved enough money to take a ship to France—a place his father had said was far more civil to black people than the United States was. In 1917 he joined the French Flying Corps and got his pilot's license—an opportunity he would not have had in the United States. No African Americans were permitted to enlist in the U.S. Air Corps, as the air force was called then, or the Marine Corps. Bullard was a skilled pilot and quickly earned the respect of the other pilots in France. He was nicknamed the "Black Swallow of Death" because of his ability to bring down German planes.

There were other Americans flying for France as well. They had come over when the world war began in 1914, three years before the United States officially entered the war. When the U.S. Air Corps joined the war in 1917, they invited all American pilots already flying for France to fly with them. Bullard requested to join, too, but was denied because he was black.

Bullard said after the war that while he had been rejected by the Americans, he knew that people everywhere were interested in his career. "I was determined to do all that was in my power to make good," he said, "as I knew the eyes of the world were watching me as the first Negro military pilot in the world."[39] He demonstrated that America's loss was France's gain as he became one of the best fighter pilots in the French Flying Corps.

"These Bonds Will Never Be Severed"

On November 11, 1918, the war finally ended with the Allies victorious, and the French commander expressed their appreciation to the African American troops who had fought with them. One French general, who had commanded the famous Red Hand Division, pledged that he and his men would always remember the 371st and 372nd black regiments who had been attached to his division. "Dear friends from America," he said, "when you have recrossed the ocean, do not forget the Red Hand Division.

After returning home from the war, soldiers from the 369th Infantry Regiment march up Fifth Avenue in New York City.

Our pure brotherhood in arms has been consecrated in the blood of the brave. These bonds will never be severed."[40]

From the U.S. Army, there were fewer appreciative words for the black soldiers. Though there were large parades in Paris to celebrate the Allied victory, American generals decided that black troops were not allowed to participate in them. In addition, many African American troops were ordered to stay in Europe to gather and bury the remains of the dead from battlefields, rebuild bridges and roads, and even load coal onto the warships that took white troops back to the United States.

One of the exceptions was the 369th, which was the first New York regiment to return home. Its troops marched up Fifth Avenue and eventually into Harlem as huge crowds lined the streets.

"A quarter of a million of men, women, and children of the colored race went wild with a frenzy of pride and joy and love," wrote one participant later. "For the final mile or so of our parade, about every fourth soldier of the ranks had a girl upon his arm—and we marched through Harlem singing and laughing."[41]

Earning the Double-Cross

While for the 369th that day was memorable, they soon learned the same lesson that all returning black troops learned after the war: the status of African Americans had not improved at all, especially in the South. The Jim Crow laws were still in place, and if anything, were even more entrenched and unyielding than before the war.

Far from being grateful to soldiers for their sacrifice, white Southerners directed a strong racial hostility at them. Many Southerners felt that black soldiers had gotten the mistaken impression from their association with the French army that they were equal to whites—and those Southerners felt it was their duty to teach the black veterans otherwise. Many returning soldiers were attacked and even killed by lynch mobs. Some of the victims were still in uniform.

In a 1918 speech in New Orleans, one Louisiana official summed up the South's position on returning black soldiers: "You niggers are wondering how you are going to be treated after the war. Well, I'll tell you, you are going to be treated exactly like you were before the war; this is a white man's country and we expect to rule it."[42]

For those who had hoped for more respect, more opportunity, and more acceptance from white America, the reality of post–World War I America was demoralizing. As one black newspaper wrote sarcastically, "For valor displayed in the recent war, it seems that the Negro's particular decoration is to be the 'double-cross.'"[43]

Chapter Four

Fighting for the Double-V

The years after World War I were violent ones for African Americans. The Ku Klux Klan became more powerful, and it stepped up its attacks on black citizens. The Jim Crow laws that made segregation between blacks and whites mandatory throughout the South were as deeply entrenched as ever. Discrimination and hostility toward African Americans had become a way of life—especially in the South.

"A Shameful Land"

Many of the returning black soldiers were unwilling to accept the racism to which they were subjected. They no longer believed that equality would be granted them if they worked hard, fought bravely, and ignored the violence and hate directed at them from white Americans. They had fought and died and been hailed as heroes by the French army. But in the United States, nothing had changed for the better.

Even black leaders such as W.E.B. DuBois, who for many years had urged black Americans to be patient, was angry at the way the veterans had been let down by the nation. He wrote in the *Crisis*:

This country of ours . . . is yet a shameful land. It lynches . . . steals . . . insults us. . . . We return from fighting. We return fighting. Make way for Democracy. We saved it in France, and by the Great Jehovah, we will save it in the U.S.A., or know the reason why. . . . We are cowards and jackasses if now that the war is over, we do not marshal every ounce of our brain and brawn to fight a sterner, longer, more unbending battle against the forces of hell in our own land.[42]

DuBois was not the only one who was angry. Not surprisingly, when some whites attempted to abuse black citizens as they had

In this 1919 photo, a mob of white children cheer after setting fire to a house in Chicago where African Americans resided.

in years past, some blacks—including veterans—fought back. For six months, beginning in the summer of 1919, there were twenty-six race riots throughout the United States. During this period, called "Red Summer" became of the bloody violence, hundreds of people were injured and killed in clashes in Washington, D.C., Chicago, and other cities around the country.

The Military Reflection

The same discrimination and inequality that existed in the society at large was mirrored in the military. There had been almost no reforms in the armed services, though African American leaders had made repeated requests for integration as well as more efficient use of black troops. The marines had not allowed blacks to join, nor had the air corps. For the vast majority of blacks in the navy, the only option was to be mess attendants—working menial kitchen or laundry detail.

The army, though open to black enlistees, also offered limited opportunities. While white soldiers were allowed to learn new skills that would help them advance in civilian life, blacks were largely used as laborers. Even more discouraging for the African American community, military leaders had a very short memory of the contributions made by black soldiers in America's wars.

As black soldiers were mustered out of the service after World War I, they were not replaced. The question that arose within the halls of the War Department was how to deal with African Americans in the event the United States waged a war in the future. Commanders from World War I weighed in with their opinions on the limited value of black troops. One of the most influential of the participants in the discussion was General W.H. Hay, who felt that black soldiers would be able to perform on the battlefield only if they were commanded by good white officers. Hay said they would be unable to function under black officers:

> On account of the inherent weaknesses in Negro character, especially lack of intelligence and initiative, it requires a much longer time of preliminary training to bring a Negro organization up to the point of training where it is fit for combat than it does in the case of white men. . . . The Negro as an officer is a failure and this applies to all classes

of Negro officers. . . . The fact that a Negro holds a commission, leaves him still a Negro with all the faults and the weaknesses of character inherent to the Negro race.[43]

Roosevelt and Black Troops

By the end of the 1930s the United States was building up its military forces again, as Europe was edging closer and closer to war. In the past, African Americans had been largely ignored until the nation went to war and needed the manpower. This time, black leaders wanted President Franklin D. Roosevelt to ensure that blacks would have more opportunities in the military. They wanted African American troops to be used as combat soldiers—as fighter pilots, as technical support personnel, and artillery gunners—instead of being relegated to labor or construction units.

Roosevelt, who had been president since 1932, had claimed to be an advocate of black equality in his campaigns. In his 1940 campaign, in which he was running for a third term, Roosevelt knew he needed African American voter support, so he made some concessions to black civil rights leaders who were demanding changes in the military. He added black advisers to the War Department and promoted Colonel Benjamin O. Davis, a veteran since the Spanish-American war, to brigadier general—the first African American ever to achieve that rank. He also assured black leaders that he supported equal opportunity for black troops in all branches of the military and promised to do something about the injustice.

The promotion of Davis and the addition of blacks to the War Department were welcome but long overdue, and civil rights leaders were not impressed—nor were they confident that Roosevelt's promise of equal opportunity in the military would actually be realized. They saw the president's actions as merely symbolic gestures rather than part of a real commitment to accomplish equality.

"The Army Is Not a . . . Laboratory"

Black leaders continued to press Roosevelt for an end to military segregation, but the president had no success in dealing with the generals of the War Department. They insisted, for a variety of reasons, that having black and white soldiers living together in

Brigadier General Benjamin O. Davis, the first African American general, is shown in London during World War II.

barracks, on warships, or serving in the same army units would prove disastrous. Some said that white troops would never stand for it, and morale would plummet. A spokesman for the generals reminded the black leaders that segregation was not the military's fault—nor was it their responsibility to fix: "The army did not create the problem. . . . The army is made up of individual citizens . . . who have pronounced views with respect to the Negro. Military orders will not change their views. . . . The army is not a sociological laboratory."[44]

But the African American community was unwilling to accept this excuse, and Roosevelt was smart enough to realize that if blacks did not enlist because of racial policies in the military, it would certainly hurt the war effort. He began to pressure military leaders in the various branches to rethink their position about the use of black troops.

A Hero Ignored

Soon after Roosevelt did so, the Japanese attacked U.S. ships at Pearl Harbor, Hawaii, on December 7, 1941. In response, Roosevelt declared war on Japan, and the United States entered World War II on the side of the Allies—the largest of which were Great Britain, France, and Russia. Ironically, the first hero of this new war was a shy twenty-two-year-old black mess attendant in the U.S. Navy who was serving on the USS *West Virginia*.

Like almost all other African Americans in the navy, Dorrie Miller spent most of his day doing menial work such as cleaning, gathering dirty laundry, and helping to prepare and serve meals. When the bombs from the warplanes hit his ship, he raced to the captain, who had been severely wounded, and moved him to a more protected area. Although Miller had never been trained to use any weapons on the ship, he grabbed a .50 caliber antiaircraft gun when the man firing it was wounded and began shooting at the incoming planes. Miller brought down at least two Japanese warplanes, although witnesses maintained that he actually hit four. "It wasn't hard," Miller said later. "I just pulled the trigger and she worked fine. I had watched the others with these guns. I guess I fired her for about fifteen minutes."[45]

In all, 130 men on the *West Virginia* were killed, and 52 were wounded, but experts said Miller's actions prevented an even greater loss of life. However, there was absolutely no mention of Dorrie Miller from the navy after this battle. When asked to describe the events on the *West Virginia* that day, navy officials referred to Miller as an "unidentified Negro messman."[46]

Not until three months later was Miller's name released, and black newspapers around the country campaigned for him to receive the Medal of Honor. The secretary of the navy and other military leaders refused, as historian Kai Wright notes, because "the navy didn't want a black poster boy."[47] Eventually, however, Dorrie Miller was awarded the Navy Cross—the first African American ever to receive that medal.

Victory at Home, Victory Abroad

When the United States declared war after the Pearl Harbor attack, African Americans turned out to enlist, although there was a different mood in the black community than there had been in past wars. This was to be a war waged not only by soldiers on battlefields around the world, but at home, too, as black citizens fought for an end to segregation and the hated Jim Crow laws. Blacks referred to the struggle as the Double-V, named after the V formed by the index and second finger, used by Allied leaders as a symbol of victory. James G. Thompson, a black cafeteria worker during World War II, explained the Double-V in a 1942 letter to the *Pittsburgh Courier:*

The Lonely Eagles

———————■———————

Even though Congress passed laws entitling African Americans to more opportunities in the armed services, in reality the military continued to drag its feet—especially when it came to training blacks to become fighter pilots. The problem, as was so often the case then, was the fear of having black and white troops training together in the same facility. Finally, with the help of First Lady Eleanor Roosevelt, who had often championed the rights of blacks, the War Department relented in 1941, allowing a separate school for black airmen at the Tuskegee, Alabama, airfield.

The school began with a class of thirteen student pilots on August 25, 1941. After seven months of grueling classroom and air training, the first cadets, including Benjamin O. Davis Jr., son of America's only black general, completed the program. The men were known as the 99th Pursuit Squadron, but they called themselves the Lonely Eagles, because they remained separate from the rest of the Air Corps.

Although many white pilots were convinced that the African American airmen would not be able to perform well in battle, they were highly successful during the 1944 invasion of Italy. In fact, the 99th Pursuit Squadron accounted for the highest number of German planes shot out of the sky. Led by Davis, the growing number of Tuskegee-trained airmen flew more than fifteen thousand missions.

Known as the Lonely Eagles, the men of the all-black 99th Pursuit Squadron listen during a training session at Tuskegee Airfield in Alabama.

The V for victory sign is being displayed prominently in all so-called democratic countries . . . then let we colored Americans adopt the double VV for a double victory. The first V for victory over our enemies from without, the second V for victory over our enemies from within. For surely those who perpetuate these ugly prejudices here are seeking to destroy our democratic form of government just as surely as the Axis forces [of Germany, Japan, and Italy].[48]

Military Segregation

Any hope that the military had abandoned its policies of segregation and discrimination soon evaporated for African American soldiers. Every barracks, every dining facility, every meeting room was organized with the idea of keeping black and white soldiers apart. On many bases in the South, buses that were supposed to shuttle soldiers back and forth to town would not allow blacks to ride. Even chapels operated under the Jim Crow laws. On most military bases they listed schedules for four services: Catholic, Jewish, Protestant, and Negroes.

Many black soldiers were furious that German prisoners of war brought back to the United States were frequently given better treatment than they were. One officer said that he and other African American soldiers at his military base had to sit in the last two rows of the base movie theater, while prisoners of war sat in front with the white Americans. At Camp Barkeley, Texas, another black soldier was appalled to observe "a sign in the latrine, actually segregating a section of the latrine for Negro soldiers, the other being used by the German prisoners and the white soldiers."[49]

One of the oddest forms of segregation had to do with the blood supplies in military hospitals. In 1941 the Red Cross, pressured by army and navy leaders, announced that its blood banks would no longer accept blood plasma donated by blacks. The reason, Red Cross officials stated, was that white men in the military "would refuse blood plasma if they knew it came from Negro veins."[50] The decision was especially ironic because a black man, Dr. Charles Drew, had pioneered the collection and storage of blood for transfusions.

"It Is a Mockery"

Although discrimination and segregation went on as before in the military, there was increased pressure from both the president and the first lady, Eleanor Roosevelt, to keep the promises made before the 1940 election. African American leaders, as well as the black press, were not willing to allow the status quo to continue, especially after Roosevelt had been so outspoken in insisting on an end to racial discrimination in the armed forces.

Though there had been an effort to allow more blacks to join the military—even branches like the marines and the air force, from which they had been banned before—military leaders consistently kept the new recruits in the same types of menial jobs they had held in other branches. One black man who had a degree in

Black marines on Iwo Jima take a break in the fighting. Black Americans served in segregated units in World War II.

biochemistry was allowed into the air force, much to his satisfaction. He did well in his training and hoped to be sent overseas. Instead, however, he was sent to another military camp, where he was made a laborer. "It is a mockery," he angrily wrote to his wife, "let no one tell you differently, this sudden opening of the so-called exclusive branches of the services to Negroes. We are trained, become skilled—and then the oblivion of common labor."[51]

The underutilization of blacks in World War II was felt not only by men, but also by black women who had joined the newly formed Women's Army Corps, or WAC. The WAC enlistees were to give support to American troops as secretaries, stenographers, telephone operators, and even ambulance drivers. Black WACs, however, were disappointed to learn that instead of providing such services, they mopped, swept, and scrubbed—sometimes even for white WACs. At Fort Jackson, South Carolina, for example, black WACs who had extensive training as medical technicians were put to work washing walls and carrying out other menial tasks. Such assignments to women who were qualified to contribute in a more skilled capacity frequently created an atmosphere of resentment and discouragement within the ranks.

The Black Panthers of the 761st Artillery

Occasionally, however, there were exceptions—African American troops who were able to get to the front and achieve remarkable successes. The 761st Tank Battalion, whose members called themselves the Black Panthers, was one of those success stories. The battalion was formed after Roosevelt pressured the War Department to set up a few black artillery units, even though white military leaders had long maintained that black troops lacked the ability to master large artillery weapons.

Through most of the war, the 761st saw no action. They trained in the United States and experienced the usual racism and discrimination that black units faced. When they traveled by troop train to Fort Knox, Kentucky, they were told to keep the shades drawn, because white Kentuckians liked to shoot at trains carrying black soldiers. And although it seemed through the months of training that they would never see any combat at all, they got the opportunity in October 1944, when General George Patton's Third Army was pinned down by the Germans in France and needed artillery support. Because other artillery was assigned elsewhere, Patton—who had previously refused to integrate his troops—called on the 761st.

On November 2 Patton welcomed the African American troops and reminded them that they had a great deal to fight for: "Men, you're the first Negro tankers to ever fight in the American army. I would never have asked for you if you weren't good. I have nothing but the best in my army. . . . Everyone has their eyes on you and is expecting great things from you. Most of all, your race is looking forward to you. Don't let them down and damn you, don't let me down."[52]

"Why the Hell Should These Guys Fight?"

Though the German tanks were better made than the ones used by the Panthers, the Americans performed heroically. In fact, they were awarded more than 60 Bronze Stars, 12 Silver Stars, and 280 Purple Hearts. David Williams, a white captain assigned to

A Protest at Port Chicago

One of the most infamous incidents involving African American troops during World War II occurred at Port Chicago on Mare Island, California. On July 17, 1944, a large ammunition depot there exploded, and more than two hundred black sailors were killed. There was no greater loss of life on American soil during the war, and that one explosion accounted for more than 15 percent of casualties of naval personnel.

The fact that the sailors who died were black and thus had been given no other choice than being laborers enraged the black civilian community, who had been critical of the limited role of blacks in the war. When operations at the port resumed several days after the explosion, 258 African American sailors refused to work, stating that they felt that they lacked training and safety measures for such dangerous duty.

Most of the sailors, however, were eventually pressured into returning to their labor jobs at Port Chicago. Fifty who did not return were court-martialed, sentenced to hard labor for eight to fifteen years, and given dishonorable discharges. After the war their convictions were overturned. Their attorney, NAACP lawyer Thurgood Marshall, who would later become a Supreme Court justice, declared, "This is not fifty men on trial for mutiny. This is the Navy on trial for its whole vicious policy toward Negroes. . . . Negroes in the Navy don't mind loading ammunition. They just want to know why they are the only ones doing the loading!"

Quoted in Gail Buckley, *American Patriots: The Story of Blacks in the Military from the Revolution to Desert Storm*. New York: Random House, 2001, p. 310.

Wreckage was all that remained of the Port Chicago naval facility in California after a munitions explosion in 1944.

the 761st, was extremely proud of his men—especially in light of the racism they had encountered. "These guys were better than heroes," he said after the war was over, "because they weren't supposed to be able to fight, and they were treated worse than lepers. . . . I used to ask myself, why the hell should these guys fight? Why?"[53]

It was a question more and more African Americans were asking themselves as well. Though some black troops had finally had a chance to engage in combat by the end of the war, it seemed that, just as in past wars, most had been deprived of a chance to fight for their country. Many agreed with the sentiments of author James Baldwin, who noted, "The treatment accorded the Negro during the Second World War marks for me a turning point in the Negro's relation to America: to put it briefly, and somewhat too simply, a certain hope died, a certain respect for white Americans faded."[54]

Chapter Five

An Integrated Military

After suffering prejudice and discrimination in the military, almost 1 million African American veterans returned home after the war to find that there had been no improvements on the home front, either. Many had hoped that by joining the military and fighting for democracy overseas, they would make a visible contribution that would raise their status in the United States. Instead, they were viewed as they had always been—second-class citizens subject to Jim Crow laws in the South and discrimination virtually everywhere else.

Nelson Peery, who enlisted in the army after the Japanese attack on Pearl Harbor, later recalled his frustration after the war. "We went into combat because that's what we were supposed to do," he said. "And black troops have always done what needs to be done. We hoped that the residual effect would be better treatment at home after the war. We hoped that would be true. . . . [But instead] in a thousand subtle ways, in a thousand brutal ways, we were taught that we were not part of American culture and history."[55]

"Beaten and Lynched and Terrorized"

Some of these thousand brutal ways were extremely violent. It was apparent to many Southern blacks returning after the war that the Ku Klux Klan was stronger than ever and was often operating with the assent of local police. As had happened after World War I, many black veterans were beaten and even lynched —still in their uniforms.

Peery believed black veterans were targeted because they were no longer willing to occupy the lowest rung of the social ladder.

On his way to a military base for a tour of duty, a black soldier faces daily segregation in 1956 Georgia.

"The Negro troops got a taste of racial equality in foreign lands," he noted. "As they came home, that had to be beaten and lynched and terrorized out of them so they would go back to building levees and picking cotton."[56]

One of the most infamous cases of such violence involved not the Klan, but local law enforcement in South Carolina. A black sergeant named Isaac Woodard, returning home from Fort Gordon, Georgia, was scolded by the bus driver for taking too long in the "colored only" men's room along the way. The driver called the local sheriff to arrest Woodard. Though Woodard did not resist, the sheriff beat him severely with a nightstick, finally plunging the stick into the soldier's eyes, blinding him permanently.

Harry Truman, who had become president after Roosevelt died in office in 1945, believed he was aware of the problems of discrimination and racism faced by black Americans, but this incident shocked even him. "My God!" he exclaimed to civil rights leader Walter White. "I had no idea it was as terrible as that. We've got to do something."[57]

Excluded

The problems faced by African American veterans were not limited to physical violence. The postwar military leaders were rethinking the use of black troops, a process that was threatening to wipe out the gains blacks had made during World War II. Though many blacks had served with distinction at the front, those heroics were forgotten. Instead, military leaders were advocating a return to restricting black enlistees and limiting their use largely to service and labor positions.

African Americans were also excluded by many of the federal programs set up to help returning veterans. Community organizations such as the American Legion and Veterans of Foreign Wars (VFW), which had posts in cities and towns throughout the United States, were designated "white only," although blacks were sometimes issued limited memberships in separate facilities. Other programs were difficult for blacks to use simply because of segregation in society as a whole. For instance, the G.I. Bill, which was a way of helping veterans pay for college, was often useless to blacks because so many universities were open to white students only. And the strict segregation of neighborhoods meant that G.I.

loans for black veterans to use for purchasing a home could be used only in all-black communities.

Executive Order 9981

Such discrimination was unacceptable to African Americans, who were fed up with the government's slow pace in dealing with their problems. Though Truman supported civil rights for all Americans, he was first and foremost a politician, and was wary of committing to any course of action that could cost him votes in the upcoming 1948 presidential election. Only when he became convinced that the large bloc of black voters in the Northern states would vote Republican against him did Truman tackle the U.S. military.

On July 26, 1948, he issued what was known as Executive Order 9981, in which he called for an end to segregation in all branches of the military:

> It is essential that there be maintained in the armed service of the United States the highest standards of democracy, with equality of treatment and opportunity for all those who serve in our country's defense. It is hereby the policy of the President that there shall be equality of treatment and opportunity for all persons in the armed forces, without regard to race, color, religion, or national origin.[58]

To oversee the progress of each of the military branches, Truman set up the Committee on Equality of Treatment and Opportunity in the Armed Forces, headed by former diplomat Charles Fahy. The Fahy Commission, as it was known, regularly reported to the president the progress or problems with implementing the order.

"As Long as I Am Commander"

While the African American community praised 9981, most military leaders did not. Some, like General Dwight Eisenhower, felt that it was impossible to combat prejudice with an executive order. "There is race prejudice in this country," he said. "When you pass a law to get somebody to like someone, you have trouble."[59]

Many commanders were concerned about the cohesiveness of military units. They worried that integrating soldiers' living, eating, and working conditions would cause disruption—something

President Harry S. Truman signs Executive Order 9981 on July 26, 1948, ending segregation in all of the United States armed forces.

that could be a dangerous distraction in combat. Despite their objections, however, the various branches of the military had no choice but to follow Truman's orders.

Still, because no exact time was specified as to when integration must occur, individual military leaders decided how quickly —or how slowly—to begin enforcing the president's order. Julius Becton Jr., a twenty-one-year-old officer in training when 9981 was announced, recalls vividly the attitude of his superior officer: "I remember the post commander assembled all the officers and he read the order to the assembled group. He then said, 'As long as I am commander here, there will be no change.'"[60]

Speeding Up Integration

The pace of integration varied from branch to branch. The air force quickly ended its restrictions on the number of blacks allowed to enlist and announced that troops would be assigned duties based on their abilities rather than their skin color. Within a year the number of African Americans was increasing in the air force by nearly five hundred men each month. The navy, too, opened up more spots for black enlistees, although it was slow to move them away from mess attendant jobs.

The marine corps and the army were far more resistant to increasing the number of black enlistees, and its leaders were more outspoken about what they saw as the dangers of integration. Though both branches made half-hearted efforts to increase the number of African Americans, they were falling far short of the goal. Both continued to allow all-black units and did not make sufficient progress in integrating either training or living facilities.

As it turned out, it was not another order from Truman or the Fahy Commision, but rather war that eventually sped up the integration process. On June 25, 1950, the Communist government of North Korea invaded South Korea. And because the United States was vehement in its condemnation of communism, Truman ordered American troops to help the South Koreans repel the invasion. Commanders at training bases throughout the United States soon found themselves overrun with untrained young men. They did not have the luxury of time in getting the recruits ready to fight, so it was a far more efficient use of space to integrate the training and living facilities.

No Longer Separate

Of course, doing away with segregation was not a smooth or easy process, even with the added impetus of war. Some commanders in the field were resolutely against integration, and they knew the Fahy Commission in Washington could do little about it if they chose to continue segregating troops in faraway Korea. However, for the most part, black and white troops fought alongside one another in the same regiments, and for the first time in U.S. history, black officers commanded white soldiers.

Charles Armstrong, who was an army sergeant during the Korean War, found himself in command of white soldiers. "Some used the 'n' word, but I got over it," he recalled. Armstrong said that at first, one white soldier repeatedly referred to him as "Nigger," but that the soldier was corrected by other white soldiers in

As a result of Executive Order 9981, blacks and whites fight side by side in an integrated infantry unit in Korea in 1950.

his troop. "[They] told him I was an officer and not to do that to me," he said. "That guy became one of my best soldiers." In the end, Armstrong said, the men realized they needed him, and that resulted in respect. "My job was being a combat officer," he recalled later. "I led the troops into combat. . . . The white soldiers . . . realized they had to follow me if they wanted to get out alive."[61]

The Korean War lasted for three years, and while as a military effort it was not as effective as Truman had hoped, it was a positive beginning to the integration of the armed forces. For example, the African American presence in the marine corps increased from only 1,075 to 15,000. The air force abandoned its all-black fighter squadrons, and began assigning black pilots wherever they were needed. The army, too, underwent a transformation, with 92 percent of black soldiers serving in integrated units.

A New Attitude

In the years following the Korean War, the civil rights movement in the United States grew stronger. With leaders such as Martin Luther King Jr., African Americans began organizing protests to fight discrimination in education, housing, and employment, especially in the South, where Jim Crow was still very much in practice.

By then, the military was the most integrated institution in the nation. Even though military pay was no way to get rich, many black soldiers said, it was steady work and allowed them to learn a skill that would hopefully get them a higher-paying job in civilian life afterward. And with the rising numbers of blacks being promoted in the service, there were many opportunities for advance-

Staying High

—————————————■—————————————

In Wallace Terry's book *Bloods: An Oral History of the Vietnam War by Black Veterans*, the author includes an account by one soldier who explained the difficulty many demoralized troops had in coping with the violence and chaos around them in a war that seemed they had no chance of winning.

In the field most of the guys stayed high. Lots of them couldn't face it. In a sense, if you was high, it seemed like a game you was in. You didn't take it serious. It stopped a lot of nervous breakdowns.

See, the thing about the field that was so bad was this. If I'm working on the job with you stateside and you're my friend, if you get killed, there's a compassion. My boss says, "Well, you better take a couple of days off. Get yourself together." But in the field we can be the best of friends and you get blown away. They put a poncho around you and send you back. They tell 'em keep moving.

We had a medic that gave us a shot of morphine anytime you want one. I'm not talkin' about for wounded. I'm talkin' about when you want to just get high. So you can face it.

Quoted in Wallace Terry, *Bloods: An Oral History of the Vietnam War by Black Veterans*. New York: Ballantine, 1984, pp. 39–40.

ment. It was not surprising, therefore, that the number of blacks in uniform increased after the Korean War, rather than diminished.

"I Feel Good About It"

While integration had been achieved in the military—making it America's racial success story—the next war, in the jungles of a small Asian nation called South Vietnam, would present a whole new set of challenges. Essentially, the United States became involved in Vietnam for the same reason it became involved in Korea. It was a means of fighting what U.S. leaders thought was the nation's most dangerous enemy—communism. President Dwight D. Eisenhower, among others, believed in the late 1950s that if Communist North Vietnam could seize South Vietnam, it would be one more step toward communism taking over the world.

At first U.S. involvement was limited to financial support for South Vietnam, as well as about seven hundred military advisers who were sent to the country to help organize and train the South Vietnamese army. However, it soon became apparent that the South Vietnamese could not fight the North alone. By the latter part of 1964, the United States had committed one hundred thousand troops to the Vietnam War.

African Americans were well represented among these troops. In fact, for the first time in history, the percentage of black troops in Vietnam was nearly the same as that of the black population of the United States—about 10 percent. They served in virtually every capacity and were awarded medals and promotions in numbers far surpassing what blacks had received in previous wars.

Such progress was heartening to black troops in Vietnam. Lieutenant Colonel George Shaffer, one of the highest-ranking black officers in the army, said, "I feel good about it. Not that I like bloodshed, but the performance of the Negro in Vietnam tends to offset the fact that the Negro wasn't considered worthy of being a front-line officer in other wars."[62]

"We Will Not Fight . . . Other People of Color"

As the presence of U.S. troops in Vietnam expanded, President Lyndon Johnson, who took office in 1963, assured the American people that the troops were there only to assist the South Vietnamese and that the war would be brief. "We are not about to send American boys nine or ten thousand miles away from home to do what Asian boys ought to be doing for themselves," he said. "We don't want to get . . . tied down to a land war in Asia."[63]

But the war dragged on, and the American public became increasingly critical of it. The war seemed to have little to do with the United States, but tens of thousands of American soldiers were being killed—and still no end was in sight. African American leaders especially criticized U.S. involvement in the conflict. Dr. Martin Luther King Jr. noted that the military was sending young black men to fight for democracy and rights that they were being denied at home. "[W]e have been repeatedly faced with the cruel irony of watching Negro and white boys on TV screens," he said, "as they kill and die together for a nation that has been unable to seat them together in the same school."[64]

Other, more militant voices insisted that because the U.S. government did not guarantee or protect black civil rights, blacks should not be drafted into the armed forces at all. One group, the Black Panther Party for Self-Defense, demanded that all black men should be exempt from military service, saying, "We will not fight and kill other people of color in the world who, like black people, are being victimized by the white racist government of America."[65]

"We All Got Drafted"

As more and more young men were drafted for the Vietnam War, the ratio of black troops to white grew significantly. One reason was that many blacks who had enlisted early on chose to reenlist—in many cases, because soldiering was a better job than they could hope for in the discriminatory civilian world.

When the war intensified, however, there was a more sinister reason for the high proportion of blacks. Increasing numbers of young men were required to report to their local draft boards, and in the South, those draft boards were almost exclusively white. Whereas during previous wars Southern draft boards had found excuses to exclude African Americans from enlisting, those same draft boards in 1967 drafted 64 percent of eligible blacks, compared to 31 percent of eligible whites.

"The thing is, a lot of white boys went to college, or graduate school," says Des, a black Vietnam veteran.

And you could get deferments for that. But in those days, not a lot of [blacks] could use graduate school or college as an out. . . . We were sent to Vietnam before we could even turn around. I think those draft boards were happy to send us over there as cannon fodder, you know, and happy to keep those white boys safe at home. That's the way it seemed to us, anyway.[66]

It is also true that many white soldiers were assigned technical and support duties—behind the lines—while the vast majority of black troops went to the front as infantry. Ironically, the combat duty sought by black soldiers in other wars as a means to prove their worth and patriotism was not as desirable in Vietnam. Not surprisingly, during much of the war, black soldiers

An African American soldier carries a wounded white serviceman on his back during heavy shelling of their cavalry unit in Vietnam.

died at a higher rate than white soldiers, too. It seemed unfair, many blacks insisted, that they should be bearing more than their share of the burden of the war.

Black and White Together

Racial strife in the United States also affected the troops in Vietnam. Many black soldiers felt the impatience with which black civilians struggled. For example, when King was assassinated in 1968, riots broke out throughout the United States, and for many black soldiers, too, already frustrated by the lack of progress in the war, this was the breaking point.

"It Was Not Their Hateful Language—It Was Ours"

In her book *We Were There: Voices of African American Veterans, from World War II to the War in Iraq*, Yvonne Latty includes an interview with Radioman James Brantley, who served in Vietnam. In this excerpt, Brantley recalls his shock at the racism he encountered in Vietnam—not by his white comrades-in-arms, but by the Vietnamese people he had come to help.

When I first got to Saigon one of the first things I saw was this toothpaste advertisement prominently placed. It was called "Light Bright" or something, and they had this little caricature of a black man, something you would see in the South, the Sambo thing. This guy is smiling with big white teeth, and that impacted me. I knew how they saw blacks based on that ad. In South Vietnam you could hear the young kids calling us "nigger." Someone else taught them that word. It wasn't a word from their culture, yet it seemed to pop up at times. I was in a bar one night and heard a Vietnamese citizen scream out "nigger" to a black GI. It was chilling, upsetting. An argument broke out after that between the two men. I had to try and stay calm, but it was hard. That ugly word was what white GIs brought to the Vietnamese people. It was not their hateful language—it was ours.

Quoted in Yvonne Latty, *We Were There: Voices of African American Veterans, from World War II to the War in Iraq.* New York: Amistad, 2004, pp. 121–23.

To honor the birthday of Martin Luther King Jr., black soldiers protest the war at a United States army base in Vietnam in 1971.

In Vietnam, many black troops in rear guard posts held protests, while some white troops jeered and taunted them with Confederate flags. In more than one case, riots resulted, according to author Michael Herr, who served in Vietnam: "The death of Martin Luther King intruded on the war in a way that no other outside event had ever done. In the days that followed, there were a number of small, scattered riots, one or two stabbings, all of it denied officially."[67]

But while such incidents could not help but divide the troops, other factors sometimes united them. "One thing I remember," says Des, "is that by 1968, nobody—nobody—thought the war could be won."

I don't even really know why we were all there. . . . The American people were against the war, and none of us in Vietnam wanted to be there either. It made for a real demoralized army. There were a lot of guys on drugs, a lot of stuff going on that had no business in the army. But nobody cared, and everybody was pissed off. What were we even doing there? White boys and black boys didn't always get along, but I guess we got together on *that*.

And when we got home from the war, you gotta understand, nobody's too wild to see soldiers. Not white, not black. The people back here looked at us as an extension of the politicians who got us into the war in the first place, the government. You'd hear about soldiers coming home, sitting in a bus depot or train station, and getting spit at by civilians. It never happened to me, but I know guys it happened to. So I guess being hated was a unifying thing. God damn, what a war.[68]

Chapter Six

Blacks in the Modern Military

Historians agree that Vietnam was definitely the lowest point in the history of American armed forces. Racial tension among the troops was but one of a number of problems in a military that was in complete disarray. It was not possible for the United States to maintain a strong military presence throughout the world with its fighting men and women as demoralized and as undisciplined as they had been during the Vietnam War. Changes had to be made, and made quickly.

Getting Rid of the "Moron Corps"

One issue that was unanimously viewed as a problem was the draft system that had been used to supply enough troops to fight the war. In 1966 it had been clear to military officials that the draft was not producing enough qualified soldiers to satisfy the rising needs in Vietnam. For one thing, draft boards were allowing more and more deferments for college and graduate students, and as a result, the pool of prospective recruits had shrunk. Johnson knew very well that abolishing such deferments would anger white middle- and upper-class voters, whose sons were the predominant recipients of such deferments.

Instead, Johnson's secretary of defense, Robert McNamara, came up with another untapped source—and even better, one that would allow the deferments to continue. McNamara's plan would enlist men who had previously been rejected—either because of physical problems or because they could not pass the mental examination necessary to enter the military. "Recruiters swept through urban ghettos and Southern rural back roads," notes author Myra MacPherson, "even taking at least one youth with an IQ of 62."[69] A little over 40 percent of the new recruits were black—almost four times the percentage of blacks in the U.S. population—largely because of the inferior education provided to blacks at the time.

Many of these recruits, both black and white, had emotional problems, anger issues, and learning disabilities. Many, too, had

Secretary of defense under Lyndon Johnson, Robert S. McNamara (shown here in 1967), increased troop numbers by recruiting young men with problems.

drug and alcohol addictions that became more pronounced during their time in Vietnam. A large percentage were incapable of taking and following orders—leading to the unkind nickname experienced soldiers used in describing the new recruits—the "Moron Corps." Though McNamara had originally promised that the new recruits would be taught technological skills that would help them get good jobs after their service was completed, in reality most were trained only for combat and were assigned to the infantry on the front lines.

Toward a Volunteer Army

It was no wonder, then, that when leaders began formulating ways to rebuild the military after Vietnam, one of the first steps was to eliminate the draft—in all of its variations. No longer would there be draft boards that during wartime would give deferments to the most privileged young men in society while blacks and other minorities would be forced to serve in their place. No more would the military be overrun with hostile, resentful troops—black or white—who did not want to serve.

The draft officially ended in 1973, when the last American troops left Vietnam. At that time the Defense Department announced its plans for what was called the All-Volunteer Force (AVF). Melvin Laird, the secretary of defense under President Richard Nixon, who had succeeded Johnson, was aware of the complaints that blacks had been historically underrepresented in combat, or, during the Vietnam war, overrepresented. Shortly before the AVF was put into place, Laird stressed that the goal was to attract young men and women of character, no matter what their race or ethnicity. "We do not foresee any significant difference between the racial composition of the All-Volunteer Force and the racial composition of the nation," he said shortly before the AVF began. "We are determined that the All-Volunteer Force shall have a broad appeal to young men and women of all racial, ethnic, and economic backgrounds."[70]

To attract what they frequently referred to as "the best and the brightest," recruiters swarmed to U.S. college campuses to talk to students. The Reserve Officers Training Corps, or ROTC, was expanded and improved. For the first time, African American colleges and universities had ROTC programs. In addition, the

"I Have No Regrets"

━━━━━━━━■━━━━━━━━

In 1991, after twenty-two years in the army, master sergeant Alex Pool wrote a letter, excerpted here, about his feelings as a black man on retiring from military life:

> After 22 years, I am retiring. I am a Vietnam veteran and would not hestitate to go to war again if called upon.
>
> We do have quality blacks [in the army]. Just look at the pictures that came out of the Persian gulf during the heat of battle. During the Vietnam War, how many blacks did you hear about [evading the draft by] going to Canada? We are a proud people, and our color never runs.
>
> I did not enlist because I could not find a job. I enlisted because my brother enlisted before me. When he came home on leave with his starched khaki uniform, jump wings, and spit-shined shoes, I knew I wanted to be a paratrooper.
>
> My mother had four sons; three served in the army. The brother I was so proud of was in Vietnam the same time I was. My mother did not ask why. She just prayed for our safe return.
>
> Sure, we have bigotry in the armed forces. However, these same bigots came from the streets of America.
>
> Although I will miss the togetherness the army instills in you to accomplish your mission, I have no regrets.

Quoted in Michael Lee Lanning, *The African-American Soldier: From Crispus Attucks to Colin Powell.* Secaucus, NJ: Birch Lane, 1997, p. 291.

military began junior ROTC programs in high schools, including those with predominantly black or Latino student bodies, to train teens in drills and military procedures and make a future in the military a more likely option for them.

Leo, who with his brother, Richard, joined the volunteer army, remembers that at the time he joined, the military was producing a number of television commercials to sell the idea of service. "It was the 'Be all that you can be' stuff—and that worked," he says.

I remember thinking, man, that looks like a good job—and not everybody could do it. It appealed to the guys who wanted to be tough and patriotic all at the same time. They made the army seem like a privilege, something you could be proud to do—rather than a ticket to hell, like the [Vietnam] vets had. It felt like you could be an American who stands up, and can show he's worth something.[71]

The pay scale was increased for every rank, and more educational opportunities than ever before were offered as a way of enticing recruits. The efforts were so successful that by 1975, every man and woman in a U.S. military uniform was a volunteer. The quality of the recruits had improved, too. By 1990, for example, 91 percent of new recruits had graduated from high school, compared with 75 percent of young people in the civilian population. New recruits were also scoring higher than ever before on military qualification tests.

Dealing with Racism in the Military

Despite the improvements, racism still existed in the military—a fact that surprised no one even though racial discrimination and segregation had been officially banned since the Korean War. After all, as Major Robert Cushman Jr. of the marines noted in 1973, while institutional racism can be eradicated with rules and changes of policy, individual racism is much more difficult to address:

Each new marine we get—whether officer or enlisted—brings along, figuratively speaking, his own personal seabag filled with the prejudices he had been collecting for eighteen years or more. The simple act of putting on a green uniform does not cause him to empty that seabag. But through training we can instill the desire in him to repack that seabag—discarding the harmful preferences and prejudices—so it does both him and fellow marines the most good.[72]

To try to eliminate racial tension on an individual level, the various branches of the military began a zero-tolerance policy of any type of racism on the part of officers. Those who felt that their own prejudices might keep them from treating every enlisted man or woman with equal respect were advised to retire quickly, and some did. Those who remained had help in becoming more racially sensitive. The military addressed the need for communication and understanding with seminars and training materials in race relations. Each unit was required to have a race relations council whose job was to consider complaints and arbitrate any problems that might arise.

Putting a New Face on the American Military

Besides these efforts to combat racism in its ranks, the post-Vietnam military also began addressing its age-old habit of promoting more whites than blacks to higher ranks. Although African Americans had received promotions more frequently during the war in Vietnam than in other wars, they tended to remain

General Daniel "Chappie" James, the only four-star black general in 1978, tells reporters that he would join the Air Force again, despite segregation in the military.

at middle ranks, while white soldiers seemed to be on a faster track to upper ranks.

That began to change in the decade after Vietnam, when talented black soldiers were finally recognized and rewarded for their service. One of the most famous was Daniel "Chappie" James, who had been a vocal opponent of segregation in the military during World War II, when he participated in a sit-in against white-only officers' clubs. Although the military frowned on this action, during the Korean War James's abilities as a fighter pilot were highly valued. He received the Distinguished Service Cross and went on to become the first black airman to lead an integrated fighter squadron. After flying more than seventy-five combat missions in Vietnam, James became the first African American four-star general in U.S. history.

Another first was the promotion of General Fred Gordon, who was appointed the first African American commandant of cadets at West Point in 1987. Gordon had fought bravely during two tours in Vietnam, and served as an Army liaison to Congress. Gordon said that blacks did benefit from the new military policy of promoting more black soldiers, although he believed that the final decision of an important post such as that at West Point was made on the basis of "professional competence on the individual level."[73] Coincidentally, Gordon's promotion occurred exactly one hundred years after Henry O. Flipper became the first black graduate of West Point.

Colin Powell's Rise to Fame

The most famous African American soldier of all was General Colin Powell, who rose through the ranks of the army to the top military position in the nation—chairman of the Joint Chiefs of Staff. The Joint Chiefs of Staff (JCS) is a panel of the highest-ranking officers of each of the military branches. As chairman of the JCS between 1989 and 1993, Powell became the main military adviser to the president of the United States and to the secretary of defense.

Powell served two tours of duty in Vietnam, where he received a medal for rescuing fellow soldiers from a helicopter crash. A strong and capable commanding officer, Powell was even more effective as a military adviser. He worked in Washington and at

As his wife, Alma, watches, General Colin Powell is sworn in as Chairman of the Joint Chiefs of Staff by defense secretary Dick Cheney in 1989.

the Pentagon for many years, helping bridge the gap between politicians and the military.

As chairman of the Joint Chiefs, Powell became the highly recognizable face of the Persian Gulf War in 1991, when he held numerous press briefings explaining what was happening in the Middle East. Unlike the war in Vietnam, the Gulf War—known in the military as Operation Desert Storm—turned out to be an extremely popular undertaking. "It was fast, and we won," says one veteran simply. "It didn't go on for years, with no mission and thousands of [casualties] like Vietnam. The bombing went on for several weeks, and the ground forces took care of business in four or five days—and minimum loss of life. Desert Storm was the American military at its best."[74]

Worry, and a Response

In the early days of the war there was some concern in the black community that Desert Storm, as well as any future wars fought by a volunteer military, would be like Vietnam, in that black soldiers would bear a greater burden in the fighting and dying than whites.

Crystal Clear

———■———

Major Anthony LaSure was part of the 177th Fighter Wing stationed in New Jersey in 2001. In this excerpt from Yvonne Latty's *We Were There: Voices of African American Veterans from World War II to the War in Iraq*, La-Sure recalls the morning of September 11 and his mission that day—and for months afterwards—preventing more attacks.

On September 11, I was . . . scheduled to fly to Fort Drum, New York, to pick up bombs and do some live exercises. I remember it like it was yesterday. It was this bright, clear morning—it was crystal clear. I thought, this is going to be such a nice day to fly. We were all on the runway taxiing and all of a sudden I got this call to come back in. Right away I think, Oh, my God, something's happened to someone's kid, because this has never happened before. . . . The chief came up to us and said a plane just rammed into the World Trade Center. . . . Then [on television] we saw the second plane crash and we got permission to take off, heading toward New York. . . .

It was the scariest thing. The Northeast corridor is the busiest airspace in the country, probably the world. . . . It's hard to get a word in edgewise as far as traffic control goes, and procedures are tight. But we took off that day and our Guard fighter planes could fly any altitude we wanted to at any airspeed. My wingman and I flew fourteen hours that day; it was a long day. We were intercepting airplanes and everyone was told to land. We were going after stragglers. . . . No one knew what was going on.

While I was flying, I compartmentalized. I didn't have time to think about the attacks or the lives that were lost. . . . For three months straight I only had twelve hours off, a day to go home, see my family, and sleep. This had never been done before—patrolling our own country.

Quoted in Yvonne Latty, *We Were There: Voices of African American Veterans from World War II to the War in Iraq*. New York: Amistad, 2004, p. 167.

One African American leader wrote a newspaper editorial in 1991 complaining that "the bulk of the fighting seems always to fall on minority groups, especially blacks and Hispanics. It's not necessarily an excuse to say that it's an all-volunteer army. If we didn't have such a racist society, the army would not be an attraction to these people who can't otherwise realize the American dream."[75]

Powell, by contrast, recalled times in American history when blacks were not allowed near the front lines but instead had to serve as labor patrols for combat troops. Now that blacks have won the right to fight, he said, it would be wrong to refuse it. More than any time in history, the peacetime military was providing opportunities and job skills to African American volunteers, and it would be wrong to refuse those, too.

"[Y]ou cannot have it both ways—favoring opportunity for blacks in the military in peacetime and exemption from risk for

Soldiers deploying for Iraq attend a farewell ceremony at Fort Stewart in Georgia. African Americans serve in all levels in today's military.

them in wartime," Powell wrote in his autobiography *My American Journey*. "There was only one way to reduce the proportion of blacks in the military: let the rest of American society open its doors to African-Americans and give them the opportunity they now enjoyed in the armed forces."[76]

Opening the Door

The modern American military has continued to work hard to ensure that racial discrimination in all its forms is eradicated. As a result, African American troops continue to serve in all levels, ranks, and branches of the military. Like Colin Powell, many of those soldiers understand that they are doing something that their forebears were prohibited from doing—fighting for their country.

Brigadier General Vincent Brooks, a veteran of the war in Iraq, says that it is crucial for African American troops to set an example both for the nation, and, especially, for other young black men and women who might consider volunteering for military service. He says:

> We have to open doors and then with one hand, reach back for others. We have come a tremendous way in the military, but we have a long way to go. . . . The military has opened the door for a whole lot of people—from the humble enlisted man who as a result gained access to education, to . . . Colin Powell, who is one of my heroes. It's not finished yet. There are doors that still have to be opened. But African Americans have always been there, in every war, meeting every challenge. We have always stood up to the call.[77]

Notes

Introduction: Struggling for the Right to Fight

1. Quoted in Jack Foner, *Blacks and the Military in American History: A New Perspective*. New York: Praeger, 1974, p. viii.

Chapter 1: Fighting for Someone Else's Liberty

2. Quoted in Foner, *Blacks and the Military*, p. 3.

3. Quoted in Kai Wright, *Soldiers of Freedom: An Illustrated History of African Americans in the Armed Forces*. New York: Black Dog & Leventhal, 2002, p. 8.

4. Quoted in Gail Buckley, *American Patriots: The Story of Blacks in the Military from the Revolution to Desert Storm*. New York: Random House, 2001, p. 11.

5. Quoted in Buckley, *American Patriots*, pp. 11–12.

6. Quoted in Michael Lee Lanning, *The African-American Soldier: From Crispus Attucks to Colin Powell*. Secaucus, NJ: Birch Lane, 1997, p. 8.

7. Quoted in Michael Lee Lanning, *Defenders of Liberty: African American Soldiers in the Revolutionary War*. New York: Citadel, 2000, p. 47.

8. Quoted in Buckley, *American Patriots*, p. 14.

9. Quoted in Ray Raphael, *A People's History of the American Revolution: How Common People Shaped the Fight for Independence*. New York: New Press, 2001, p. 254.

10. Quoted in Raphael, *A People's History*, p. 258.

11. Quoted in Raphael, *A People's History*, p. 54.

12. Quoted in Lanning, *The African-American Soldier*, p. 12.

13. Quoted in Lisa W. Strick, *The Black Presence in the Era of the American Revolution, 1770–1800*. Washington, DC: Education Department, National Portrait Gallery, Smithsonian Institution, 1973, p. 25.

14. Quoted in American Revolution.org, "The First Rhode Island Regiment of the Continental Line." www. americanrevolution.org/firstri.html.

15. Quoted in Raphael, *A People's History*, p. 287.

Chapter 2: Fighting Against a Way of Life

16. Quoted in Buckley, *American Patriots*, p. 80.

17. Quoted in Wright, *Soldiers of Freedom*, p. 60.

18. Quoted in Lanning, *The African-American Soldier*, p. 35.

19. Quoted in Lanning, *The African-American Soldier*, p. 35.

20. Quoted in Foner, *Blacks and the Military*, p. 34.

21. Quoted in Wright, *Soldiers of Freedom*, p. 60.

22. Quoted in Buckley, *American Patriots*, pp. 88–89.

23. Quoted in Lanning, *The African-American Soldier*, p. 40.

24. Quoted in Lanning, *The African-American Soldier*, pp. 46–47.

25. Quoted in Lanning, *The African-American Soldier*, p. 41.

26. Quoted in William Kashatus, "Fifty-Fourth Massachusetts Regiment," History Net.com. www.thehistory net.com/ah/blglory/index.html.

27. Quoted in Buckley, *American Patriots*, p. 98.

28. Quoted in Foner, *Blacks and the Military*, p. 42.

29. Quoted in Buckley, *American Patriots*, p. 104.

Chapter 3: Over Here and over There

30. Quoted in Gerald Astor, *The Right to Fight: A History of African Americans in the Military*. Novato, CA: Presidio, 1998, p. 46.

31. Quoted in Wright, *Soldiers of Freedom*, p. 114.

32. Quoted in Foner, *Blacks and the Military*, p. 88.

33. Quoted in Foner, *Blacks and the Military*, p. 76.

34. Quoted in Spartacus, "First World War: Afro-American Soldiers." www.spar tacus.schoolnet.co.uk/FWWafro.htm.

35. Quoted in Bernard C. Nalty, *Strength for the Fight: A History of Black Americans in the Military*. New York: Free Press, 1989, p. 107.

36. Quoted in Foner, *Blacks and the Mlitary*, p. 117.

37. Quoted in Foner, *Blacks and the Military*, p. 117.

38. Quoted in Astor, *The Right to Fight*, pp. 114–15.

39. Quoted in Buckley, *American Patriots*, p. 173.

40. Quoted in Arthur W. Little, *From Harlem to the Rhine: The Story of New York's Colored Volunteers*. New York: Covici, Friede, 1936, p. 350.

41. Little, *From Harlem to the Rhine*, p. 362.

42. Quoted in Lanning, *The African-American Soldier*, p. 151.

43. Quoted in Arthur E. Barbeau and Florette Henri, *The Unknown Soldiers: African-American Troops in World War I*. Philadelphia: Temple University Press, 1974. 174.

Chapter 4: Fighting for the Double-V

44. Quoted in Lanning, *The African-American Soldier*, p. 151.

45. Quoted in Astor, *The Right to Fight*, pp. 126–27.

46. Quoted in Lanning, *The African-American Soldier*, p. 170.

47. Quoted in Wright, *Soldiers of Freedom*, p. 155.

48. Quoted in Buckley, *American Patriots*, p. 275.

49. Wright, *Soldiers of Freedom*, p. 155.

50. Quoted in Buckley, *American Patriots*, p. 257.

51. Quoted in Astor, *The Right to Fight*, p, 184.

52. Quoted in Foner, *Blacks and the Military*, p. 140.

53. Quoted in Foner, *Blacks and the Military*, p. 147.

54. Quoted in Gina Di Nicolo, "Come Out Fighting," *Military Officer*, February 2006, p. 66.

Chapter 5: An Integrated Military

55. Quoted in Maggi M. Morehouse, *Fighting in the Jim Crow Army: Black Men and Women Remember World War II*. Lanham, MD: Rowman & Littlefield, 2000, p. 201.

56. Quoted in Morehouse, *Fighting in the Jim Crow Army*, p. 202.

57. Quoted in www.teachingamerican history.org/library/ubdex.asp?docu ment+591.

58. Quoted in Lanning, *The African-American Soldier*, p. 221.

59. Quoted in Foner, *Blacks and the Military*, p. 181.

60. Quoted in Yvonne Latty, *We Were There: Voices of African American Veterans, from World War II to the War in Iraq*. New York: Amistad, 2004, p. 77.

61. Quoted in Latty, *We Were There*, p. 58.

62. Quoted in Foner, *Blacks and the Military*, p. 205.

63. Quoted in American President.org, "Lyndon Baines Johnson (1963–1969), Biography: Foreign Affairs." www. american president.org/history/ lyndonbjohnson/biography/foreign affairs.common.shtml.

64. Quoted in Lanning, *The African-American Soldier*, p. 256.

65. Quoted in Wright, *Soldiers of Freedom*, p. 226.

66. Des, interview with author, June 16, 2006, Richfield, Minnesota.

67. Quoted in Buckley, *American Patriots*, p. 409.

68. Des, interview with author.

Chapter 6: Blacks in the Modern Military

69. Myra MacPherson, "McNamara's 'Moron Corps,'" *Salon.com*, May 29, 2002. www.salon.com/news/feature/ 2002/05/20/mcnamara/index.html.

70. Quoted in Lanning, *The African-American Soldier*, p. 277.

71. Walter White, *A Man Called White*. Athens: University of Georgia Press, 1995, p. 331.

72. Leo, interview with author, June 14, 2006, Minneapolis, Minnesota.

73. Quoted in Lanning, *The African-American Soldier*, p. 275.

74. Quoted in Buckley, *American Patriots*, p. 441.

75. Roger, interview with author, April 22, 2006, Minneapolis, Minnesota.

76. Quoted in Lanning, *The African-American Soldier*, p. 284.

77. Colin Powell, *My American Journey*. New York: Random House, 1995, p. 501.

78. Quoted in Latty, *We Were There*, pp. 180–81.

For More Information

Books

Michael L. Cooper, *Hell Fighters: African-American Soldiers in World War I*. New York: Lodestar, 1997. Helpful index and bibliography.

Jim Haskins, *Black, Blue & Gray: African Americans in the Civil War*. New York: Simon & Schuster, 1998. Good section on the South's refusal to allow black soldiers.

Brenda Moore, *To Serve My Country, To Serve My Race: The Story of the Only African American WACs Stationed Overseas During World War II*. New York: New York University Press, 1996. Very interesting first-person accounts, helpful endnotes.

Wallace Terry, *Bloods: An Oral History of the Vietnam War by Black Veterans*. New York: Ballantine, 1984. Explicit and gritty reading, but excellent way to understand the emotions of soldiers on the front lines in Vietnam.

Web Sites

African American Odyssey (http://memory.loc.gov/ammam/ aaohtml/exhibit/aointro.html). This site contains information from the Library of Congress about the history of blacks in the United States, both in the military and civilian life. Excellent sections on the Civil War and Jim Crow eras, with photographs and helpful visual aids.

Guide to Black History (http://search.eb.com/blackhistory/ micro/179/2.html). This site includes a large number of articles and biographies about African Americans in the military, as well as black civilian leaders who pushed for integration of the armed forces.

History of Black Military Service (www. redstone.army.mil/history/integrate/ history.htm). A very complete site tracing achievements by black troops from colonial times to World War II.

Index

Picture Credits

Cover, Time Life Pictures/Getty Images

© Bettmann/CORBIS, 41, 43, 47, 50, 53, 56, 63, 66, 69, 75, 77, 84, 86

© Joseph Scwartz/CORBIS, 60

© Peter Turley/CORBIS, 88

© CORBIS, 11, 14, 21, 25, 27, 30, 35, 71

Hulton Archive/Getty Images, 33, 36, 45, 59

Time Life Pictures/Getty Images, 80

Library of Congress, 7, 13, 24, 38, 52, 65, 79

North Wind Picture Archives, 19, 40

About the Author

Gail B. Stewart received her undergraduate degree from Gustavus Adolphus College in St. Peter, Minnesota. She did her graduate work in English, linguistics and curriculum study at the College of St. Thomas and the University of Minnesota. She taught English and reading for more than ten years.

She has written over ninety books for young people, including a series for Lucent Books called The Other America. She has written many books on historical topics such as World War I and the Warsaw ghetto.

Stewart and her husband live in Minneapolis with their three sons, Ted, Elliot, and Flynn; two dogs; and a cat. When Stewart is not writing, she enjoys reading, walking, and watching her sons play soccer.